Creative Time & Space

Making Room for Making Art

Ricë Freeman-Zachery

NORTH LIGHT BOOKS

Cincinnati, Ohio

www.mycraftivity.com
Create. Connect. Explore.

14 13 12 11 10   5 4 3 2 1

Distributed in Canada by Fraser Direct
100 Armstrong Avenue
Georgetown, ON, Canada L7G 5S4
Tel: (905) 877-4411

Distributed in the U.K. and Europe by David & Charles
Brunel House, Newton Abbot, Devon, TQ12 4PU, England
Tel: (+44) 1626 323200, Fax: (+44) 1626 323319
E-mail: postmaster@davidandcharles.co.uk

Distributed in Australia by Capricorn Link
P.O. Box 704, S. Windsor, NSW 2756 Australia
Tel: (02) 4577-3555

Library of Congress Cataloging-in-Publication Data

Freeman-Zachery, Ricë.
   Creative time and space / Rice Freeman-Zachery. -- 1st ed.
      p. cm.
   Includes bibliographical references and index.
   ISBN-13: 978-1-60061-322-7 (pbk. : alk. paper)
   ISBN-10: 1-60061-322-5 (pbk. : alk. paper)
   1. Art--Psychology. 2. Creation (Literary, artistic, etc.) I. Title.
   N71.F656 2009
   701'.15--dc22
                              2009011303

Editor
Tonia Davenport

Designer
Geoff Raker

**Production
Coordinator**
Greg Nock

Photographer
Adam Hand

www.fwmedia.com

Dedication

To Earl; without whom, nothing

In Memorium

Betty Burks Freeman: June 9, 1926–August 11, 2006
Rice Calvin Freeman: July 28, 1926–July 27, 2008

Acknowledgments

Where to start when you have so many people to thank? First, of course, I heartily thank the artists who contributed not only their art but their ideas, tips, and encouragement. They answered dozens of my nosy questions and met difficult deadlines, all in the spirit of sharing what they've discovered so the rest of us can make the most of our own creativity.

Thank you to my two terrific editors, Tonia Davenport and Jessica Strawser, whose vision and hard work made this book concrete. They and the team at North Light Books are simply the best.

Thanks to all the wonderful, fabulously talented, and hilariously funny people who take time out of their days to stop by my blog. They have created the artistic community I've always wanted. When I started my blog, I had no idea what wonderful people would show up to entertain me, cheer me on, offer ideas and information, and encourage me to laugh every day. Y'all are fabulous!

Thank you to Karen, Paula, Roz, and Wendy: the members of WWSF (loosely translated—Women Who Say a Very Bad Word That Would Make Your Mother Cringe). These are the smartest, funniest, most opinionated women on the planet, and I'm lucky to know them. For any question I could possibly have, one of them is sure to know the answer, whether I'm asking about gouache or Goya, math or menopause, or the name of that animal that isn't a raccoon.

And, as always, I owe everything to my husband, Earl. To say he's supportive sounds as if he merely puts up with me. The truth is that he thinks everything I do is marvelous (well, most everything) and thinks I'm funny (most of the time) and suggests ideas and approaches that I hadn't even thought of. He retired at 55 and took over all of the cooking and house-work (not that I ever did a whole lot of either of those) to give me more time to create. Any wonder why my books are dedicated to him? I think not.

Contents

Introduction

Perhaps creating keeps you young. There is no time when you are in the creating space. The more of this world's time that you spend there, the less you age.

—David Mack, *Kabuki: The Alchemy*

From the time I was a little kid until well into adulthood, I kept my Important Stuff in a green Army portable field desk. It held pens and paper and notebooks and, later on, art supplies. Wherever I moved, the desk moved with me; and everything I needed was neatly stored in its drawers.

Today I work at one of three long tables in my office (one of three rooms in our house devoted to writing and making art). I look at my old field desk (tucked away in storage) and marvel that, for so many years, everything I needed fit into a space smaller than a suitcase.

What happened to make me need so much more space? And what happened to make me feel so pressed for time? I can remember being a kid—back in the days when that Army desk held a pink flowered notebook and a box of crayons—and feeling summer afternoons stretching out into infinity. Not anymore. Time, just like space, has become a mystery to me. Is it a mystery for you, too?

You know the feeling: You're working on something that's finally coming together for you. Or maybe it's not, not quite yet, but you can sense that it's getting there. You're in the zone, deep in concentration, making the connections. Finally you come up for air, take a little break. You glance up at the clock and do a double take. Hours have passed without your being aware of it. The afternoon has slipped into evening. Isn't that a marvelous feeling? And don't you wish you could get there more often—to that timeless space where you can immerse yourself in your work without having to watch the clock? It's just like it was when you were a kid and had those long, long afternoons in July stretching out before you, timeless and endless and full of possibility.

We all battle time. We think we need more, we wish it would pass more quickly, we postpone doing things in the hope that time will slow down enough that we never actually have to tackle them. Artists, especially, have a complicated relationship with time. And when we think about time, we automatically think about space. At least I do. Time and space are two things I'm always coveting. Do you ever think about how much more creative you would be if you had just a couple more hours in every day? Or how much more you could get done if you had your very own studio where you could leave everything just as it was at the end of the day and walk out and close the door?

You are, of course, far from being alone. In fact, you're in very, very good company, indeed. There may be a few artists somewhere who have all the time and all the space they could possibly need, but I sure haven't talked to them. The artists I talk to—even the ones who make art full time in custom-designed studios—all could use just a little more.

Time and space are always issues, no matter what creative work you do. And when we talk about time and space, we aren't talking just about clock time and actual physical space. That would be the easy part. If that were all there was to it, we could cut out all the chores and errands and let the house and yard work pile up in order to gain a few extra hours a week; and we could scrimp and save and add a little room onto the back of our house where we could actually go to paint.

But it's not that easy, because when we talk about "time," we're talking about the way we perceive time and how we feel about the time we have. We're talking about obligations and the way we divide our days into "work time" and "leisure time" and "family time" and all the ways we juggle the things we have to get done in any twenty-four-hour period.

And when we talk about "space," we're talking not only about the physical space we inhabit, but also about the space—the amount of room, the imaginary space—inside our heads that's allotted to our art. If we could divide our brains like pies, most of us would have big thick slices for obligations, like work and chores and dental appointments. We'd have slightly smaller slices for friends and family, and still smaller slices for everything else, things like dropping off the dry-cleaning, car-pooling, preparing meals, sleeping and flossing our teeth; and, somewhere in there, we might have a little sliver—the size you cut for yourself just after your annual physical and that moment of reckoning when you step on the nurse's scale—for making art. Many of us simply don't give a lot of the space in our brains to thinking about the art we make.

Remember how it was the first time you fell in love? It was all you could think about. You were working at a job or going to school (or both), eating meals and getting lots of things done, but, in your head, it was All Love, All the Time.

Why can't it be like that with your art? Why can't it consume your brain just the way love did? You could still get everything done and be present in meetings and at dinners with friends; but in your mind, you'd always be thinking about art, about ideas and inspiration and what you were going to do next.

Why not? It's like that for lots of people. The artists here are going to tell you that their art consumes them. It's what they're thinking about when they wake up, and it's what lulls them to sleep (or not) at night. It's always there, filling the space inside their heads.

Do they still wish they had more? Of course they do. They understand what it's like to need more time and more space. But they also understand about making it work, no matter how many hours you have to devote to your art or how much space you have—or don't have—to spread out your supplies. Sure, it's about eking out an hour and clearing off the kitchen table; but, even more, it's also about rethinking your approach to the hours in every day and the space inside your head. It's about making art important and putting it up there with the other things you hold dear. Your family and friends love you; they won't mind sharing you with the work that makes your soul sing.

7

Meet the Artists

Traci Bautista

Traci Bautista is a mixed-media artist, designer, teacher and author. She designs (Kōl LäJ), an eclectic line of paper art kits, and teaches workshops around the world. Traci is the author of *Collage Unleashed* and writes for various mixed-media publications. Her artwork has been featured in magazines and books and on HGTV and DIY. In 2008, Traci launched Collage Pauge, a line of collage adhesives, papers and tools. To learn more about her artwork, events, and creative musings, visit www.treicdesigns.com or her blog at http://kollaj.typepad.com.

Theo Ellsworth

Theo Ellsworth is a self-taught artist and author living in Portland, Oregon. His first book, *Capacity*, is a 336-page hand-drawn graphic novel that documents events that actually took place inside of the author's head. He is incredibly fond of impossible objects, preposterous notions and imaginary animals. You can find more of his work at www.artcapacity.com.

PHOTO BY TRACY V. MOORE

Lisa Lichtenfels

Lisa Lichtenfels is a fabric sculptor living in Springfield, Massachusetts. Her work can be seen at the CFM Gallery, 112 Greene Street, New York, NY 10012. For information, call 212-966-3864 or e-mail: info@cfmgallery.com. You can see more of her work online at www.lisalichtenfels.net, and you may contact Lisa at lisalichtenfels@comcast.net or P.O. Box 90537, Springfield, MA 01139-0537.

Chris Malone

Chris Malone is an artist living in Washington, D.C. When he is not working, you will find him with his four birds and four dogs, and his partner, Bill. You can reach him at chrismalone162@msn.com, and you can see more of his work at www.cmaloneyart.com.

Thomas Mann

Thomas Mann describes himself as an artist working in the medium of metal—more a sculptor than a jeweler. A self-employed artist since 1970, he is best known for his Techno-Romantic Jewelry Objects®, a style he invented in the late 1970's and pursued intensely over the next twenty years. Since the turn of the century, he has moved away from his signature Techno-Romantic® design vocabulary toward edgier jewelry designs that are, in some cases, models for large-scale sculpture. You can check out what Tom's up to by visiting www.thomasmann.com. If you're in New Orleans, stop by Thomas Mann Gallery I/O at 1810 Magazine Street or call 504-581-2111.

Teesha Moore

Teesha Moore is a visual-journal artist living in Issaquah, Washington. She has organized Artfest—a 600-person alternative art retreat—for the past ten years, and Artfiberfest for five. A new retreat called Journalfest debuted in October 2009. She also teaches at several smaller retreats, has spent the last twelve years publishing a funky art magazine, and has run a rubber stamp company called Zettiology for fifteen years. However, she still takes time to journal every day, as she feels it is her secret to success. You can reach her at artgirl777@aol.com or see more at www.teeshamoore.com.

Judy Coates Perez

Judy Coates Perez is a mixed-media textile artist in Chicago, Illinois. One part gypsy, two parts visual alchemist, Judy believes the diverse places she has lived are manifested in her work. Exploring themes from folklore, history, and nature, she enjoys working in a variety of media, often blending quilting skills with techniques from her graphic arts background. Judy uses textile paints, dyes, inks, acrylic powders, and artist's pencils and occasionally stitches metal onto her fabric. This creative restlessness mirrors her life experience. You can reach her at judycoatesperez@gmail.com, and you can see more of her work at www.judyperez.blogspot.com.

Kelly Rae Roberts

Kelly Rae Roberts is a mixed-media painter, author and possibilitarian living in Seattle, Washington. She is the author of *Taking Flight: Inspiration + Techniques to Give Your Creative Spirit Wings*, a popular arts and craft book that encompasses all aspects of what it means to live the creative life. Her work has been featured in a variety of mixed-media books by her peers, and she's had several articles published in various magazines, including *Cloth Paper Scissors* and *Memory Makers*. Recently, she signed on with Brush Dance Publishing and Demdaco for long-term licensing agreements that will showcase her work on cards, journals, magnets, calendars and decorative wall art in stores nationwide. You can learn more about her at www.kellyraeroberts.com.

Pam RuBert

Pam RuBert is an artist living in Springfield, Missouri. She shares an art studio inside an old renovated peanut butter factory with her husband and sculptor Russ RuBert, their dog Mochi, and, at last count, fifty-three vintage mannequins. After working in painting, ceramics, illustration, and animation, Pam started making art quilts in 2004. Since then her quilts have been featured on PBS, and in Quilt National, FiberArts International, and other exhibitions touring the United States, Europe, Asia, and Africa. You can reach her at pam@rubert.com and see more of her work at www.pamrubert.com.

Lori Marsha Sandstedt

Lori Sandstedt designs recycled fashion and accessories in Redlands, California. Her clothing line, Lorimarsha, marries collaged couture with environmental responsibility. Her use of vintage textiles imprint her clothing with a sense of history, mixing modern and vintage in a way that defies category classifications. You can email her at lori@lorimarsha.com and see more of her work at www.lorimarsha.com.

Carter Seibels

Carter Seibels lives a life full of beads with her soul mate and bead partner, Aveesh, and the world's best golden retriever, Finn. When she's not knee-deep in beads, you can find Carter dabbling in other creative ventures, walking with Finn, reading a book, or enjoying one of her many favorite foods. You can reach her at ctseibels@gmail.com and see more of her work at www.divaliglassjewelry.com.

Susan Sorrell

Susan Sorrell is a mixed-media artist in Greenville, South Carolina. She has been working with textiles since 1998, combining painting, sewing, beading, and embellishing on fabric. Her recent series of work, "Southern Fried Fiber," is inspired by her southern roots. To view more of Susan's work, visit her Web site www.creativechick.com.

Roz Stendahl

Roz Stendahl is a graphic designer, book artist, and mixed-media artist in Minneapolis, Minnesota. She's a third culture kid who has spent her whole life writing and drawing her observations of the world. "I don't know any other way to live. Observing folks (and animals), dressing comfortably (you never know when you'll be chased by spies), being as productive as possible, and encouraging people to be productive, too—I guess it can all be reduced down to that. Those are the tenets of my life." You can find out more about Roz at www.rozworks.com and www.rozwoundup.typepad.com.

Judy Wise

Judy Wise is a painter and mixed-media artist living in Canby, Oregon. She is an international art and creativity teacher and has been writing, painting, printmaking, and journaling all her life. You can reach her at judywise@canby.com, and you can see more of her work at www.judywise.com and on her blog at www.judywise.blogspot.com.

Creative Time

Time. What is time, anyway? Is it an actual thing, like water or a rock? Or is it an artificial construct that we've invented and use only because we need to be able to schedule things like board meetings and basketball practice? I'm going to argue the only thing about time that's really important is how you think about it; and then I'm going to have really creative people tell you how they make time work for them and how you can do that, too. Time doesn't have to be the enemy, the Bad Boss, the thing lurking around the corner as you're sitting at the easel or the potter's wheel, waiting to leap on you and harangue you about the garbage that needs to be taken out right this minute. Time can, instead, be an ally, stretching and flexing to allow you the opportunity to get in your studio and make something without keeping one eye on the clock. (And what are you doing with a clock in your studio, anyway? If you must, set a timer and put it out of sight. Ignore it until it goes off.)

We're going to look at two kinds of time—measured and perceived. First, in Chapters 1 and 2, we'll talk about actual hours, about what fills your days and how to weed out the things that are eating up time but not giving you anything you really need. The artists will tell you how they make more time, what they cut out and what they avoid; and we'll offer suggestions for how you can start changing what's consuming your days. In Chapter 3, we'll talk about organization and structure, and you'll begin to think about how much of this you need in your own life—it varies for everyone, and there's no single right way to approach it. Fortunately for all of us, the artists here have lots of different ideas, no two alike. But, knowing artists, you guessed that, right?

Then we'll shift a little, and we'll talk about how time *feels* to you, and what you put into the hours you have. When you have a big chunk of time in front of you, a space of several hours in your studio, what happens? Do you have trouble getting started? In Chapter 4, we'll talk about that feeling of, well—dare we call it boredom? Maybe. Or maybe it's just a kind of fear of getting started. Whatever it is, we'll offer tips to get past it.

Or maybe you find yourself stuck in time, spinning your wheels and doing the same thing over and over and over, like a repeating Art Machine. In Chapter 5 you'll find stories about getting past the ruts and tips for making that happen. It's about where to find inspiration for something new and how to move on from cranking out what feels like the same old stuff, month after month, year after year.

However you look at time, this first section will help you figure out ways to make the most of what you've got. Tips and stories, ideas and inspiration—it's enough to make even Father Time feel all warm and fuzzy.

Chapter 1

Exploring Time

What Exactly Does "Time" Mean to You?

In my house I have a clock that is perpetually slow. I put in new batteries and reset it; but, within a day, it's right back to its slacker ways. I should just buy a new clock, but I kind of like this one. When I go into that room, it's as if I've been given a gift, a little bonus of time. Ten minutes isn't much, in the larger framework of a day, but it's enough to write a sentence or two, check e-mail, even put in a load of laundry or brush on a coat of gesso. Whenever I'm feeling particularly rushed for time, I can go into the room with the lazy clock and take a deep breath and think, "Ah. There's plenty of time." And it turns out that this is true.

Perhaps you've been thinking you're the only person who fervently wishes for more hours in the day to be creative—just thirty minutes in the morning before work, maybe a couple of hours after dinner in the evening. *Au contraire*. You are most definitely not alone. You're in excellent company: The irritatingly persistent lack of time is one of the most common laments I hear from creative people everywhere, all of whom so desperately wish there were some way to do all the things that have to be done—the day job, the cleaning, the laundry, the childcare, not to mention the nonessentials such as, say, eating and sleeping—and still have just a little time to paint or stitch or sculpt or write. They all imagine that if art were their life, their Real Job, everything would fall easily into place.

That, of course, is not the case. Even when making art is your Real Job, everything else still has to be done. Working artists will remind you that if you're making a living at making art, you're not only making the art, but you're selling the art and packing and shipping the art. Maybe you're showing the art at fairs and in galleries, or maybe you're running an online shop. You do the marketing and the self-promotion, the billing and the banking, the public relations and the interviews. All of those other, non-actual-art-making things take up way more time than you can imagine because you're doing them all yourself, often

Art Watch—Pam RuBert

learning as you go. Pam and Carter both spend much of their days working at other art-related businesses with their partners. Judy Perez has two home-schooled children at home, so they're with her all day long. Thomas has fifteen employees and spends about two-thirds of every year on the road, traveling to workshops and shows and meetings. They're all successful artists, but there's not a single one of them who has the luxury of never having to wrangle time. Not one has the option of spending every day in the studio doing nothing but making art. No one does, except in a movie fantasy where the artist has a staff of people who take care of every single thing from tying her shoes to running the bath water to fielding requests for interviews.

What everyone else has is a chance to find time for art, somewhere. It's hard to imagine how working artists do it without full-time help and a secret formula for adding extra hours to their days. Finding time to make art feels so very difficult that we can't even imagine where to start.

Enough—Kelly Rae Roberts

Try This

Stop and think about all the things you do during the day. Make a list of your usual activities, using two columns. On the left, list all the things you think of as left-brain, non-creative, routine: work, shopping, paying bills, helping with homework. On the right, list all the creative things you do: painting, sketching, writing in your journal. Prop it up where you can look at it. You don't need to do anything else with it right now.

It is not bleak and hopeless, however. One of the first things you have to do with any job where you're your own boss—whether it's making art or making tacos or leading midnight ghost tours through the French Quarter—is to figure out what "time" means to you and how to establish a good relationship with it. Working artists know this, and they all have their own quirky ways of thinking about time.

It's a conundrum, for sure. Ideally, you want unlimited time for creativity, with no clocks and no schedules to interrupt its flow. But in an ideal relationship with time, you would also have some way to make sure everything gets done. Is there a solution? Sure there is. In fact, there are several, depending on how your brain works and how you feel about time itself.

One possibility that creative people embrace has less to do with ignoring time and more to do with re-thinking how we imagine time. In Alan Lightman's wonderful book *Einstein's Dreams*, the author presents fantasies about time that look nothing like the way we think of "time" and its habits. In some, time is circular. In others, time never moves, or it moves backward. The reviews of the book (quite excellent, laudatory reviews) refer to Einstein and his imagination and the ways in which he thought more like an artist than a scientist—at least about things like time. Perhaps that is the key: to learn to think about time as artists do. And just how might that be?

Roz explains one way of doing this, saying, "I think that all the artists I know do view time differently than

non-artists in the sense that the artists I know all have a sense of the futility of time that comes from stepping fully into the present moment and creating something. You get so absorbed in what you are doing that time as conventionally measured just ceases to exist. Time becomes very full and rich in ways I don't feel capable of explaining. It's like a deep, full, calm breath.

"The healthy side effect of stepping into this sense of time is you can't worry about the past or fret about the future. It would be lovely to live there all the time. I'm not there, but I try to get there as often as possible. When I teach journaling, I spend a lot of time talking about this sense of time. Those who start to build a daily practice really come to understand it." While it would be ideal, as Roz says, to stay in this timeless zone all day every day, that isn't possible for most people. Still, there are ways to learn how to step into that zone whenever you have a chance. (Regular journaling is certainly one way, and you'll find out lots more about that in Chapter 7.)

Try This

How do you think of time? First, draw a "time line" for a typical day—and it doesn't have to be a line. Draw a line or a circle or triangle or whatever—that represents how you see time. Make it thin in the parts where time seems to fly by, and make the line thicker in the parts of the day when it seems to slow down. Place hash marks at the points of the day that divide one part from another. Yours might lie at mealtimes and breaks, or they might mark the delineation between home life and work or between the times when your brain is sluggish and when it's perking. Add as many details as you want to create a visual representation of how you see time. Pin this up where you can study it. How does it make you feel: Rushed? As if you have plenty of time? Make notes about these perceptions in your notebook.

November 25. 2007
Week One. Bird A Day paintings
Acrylic on canvases I have...
Top left to right 1 to 5 (which
is on top of scansog #6).
Bottom left: Sketches, #6 + #7,
Then a pile of canvases + just
one portion of my chickadee
sketch showing (for tomorrow)
These are on the table in the studio
back to back with my computer—
hence the wires.
1–3, +7 are on 6x12 (12x6)" canvas.
4 is on a 6x6 canvas. 5 is on an 8x8"
Square canvasboard. 6 is on an 8x10"
canvas board.
I was holding the camera up above
the table... but even without great
focus I like seeing them all and
the approaches I tried. I want to
get looser and I want a little
more humor.
The copier is broken so I'm having to scan
my sketches into Photoshop—then
put them into Quark to plan work + cropping.

Bird-a-Day Journal—Roz Stendahl

For those of us used to living by clock time, where there are certain hours for breakfast and work, lunch and breaks and dinner, then bedtime, this can seem quite amazing. We sit at a desk and, without even thinking about it, glance up every five or fifteen or thirty minutes, unconsciously checking the passage of time. Maybe it's creeping because you're tired of writing proposals and want to go to the gym, or maybe it's flying past because you've got to get these invoices out today. Either way, though, you're doing what we all have learned to do: adapting your day, your work, your life, to the passage of what we perceive as "time."

Is it possible to change how we do that? After talking to dozens of the most creative people on the planet, I believe it is. I believe it's possible to forge a relationship with time that takes away its power to intimidate us and, instead, turns it into an ally in our pursuit of creativity.

Try This

Make a list of things you do where you lose track of time. Start with* sleeping, *just to get the ball rolling. List everything you can think of, even if it's something you've done only once*—walking on the beach in Hawaii at sunrise, *or* hang gliding*—in addition to the times you've lost track of time in your studio. If you can, remember exactly what it was that captured your mind so completely. Was it a difficult part of a painting, where you were forced into intense concentration? Or was it when things were going really smoothly and your hands were flying and you looked up from the sewing machine or the easel and found time had left you? What seems to be instrumental into moving your brain into that state of being outside of time? Make a list of those things. Once you have an idea of what causes that sidestep, you can work to incorporate more of that into your day. If intense concentration seems to do it, you'll want to give yourself problems to solve. If smoothly flowing handwork does it, well, you know what to do.

Teesha says, "I suppose artists view time differently in that it seems to lose meaning when you are in the throes of creativity. It doesn't seem to matter—actually nothing else really matters if you are fully present in your creative stream-of-consciousness. It's an addicting state to be in. Time needs to feel organic—that we are using it for our purposes and not it using us." Rather than keeping one eye on the clock and cringing at the movement of the hands—too slow, too fast—we can learn to step outside of clock time and make use, instead, of our own flow of energy—as energetic time—to get things done.

Theo explains, "The question that people ask me the most is how long it takes me to draw a picture. I suppose this makes me feel like I do have a different relationship with time because I never have an answer. It's actually never felt important to me to figure out how long a piece takes to finish. I just do it. Losing track of time is part of what makes the process worth it to me. I get to disappear into the process for a while. I like the way my thoughts flow while I'm engaged in drawing. I remember a lot of dreams and childhood moments while I'm working, and I don't feel like time really has any place in the process. Art is a way to sidestep time and feel timeless for a while."

Ahhh. . . That's a wonderful feeling, indeed. You've felt it, surely, when you're engrossed in a project, doing something you love. It's exactly like you've sidestepped time and slid over into some other realm where nothing matters but the process. And where, it turns out, you're in really good company.

Judy Perez says, "There is nothing better than sitting down to work on something and finding that five hours have gone by, and you thought it was barely an hour. I think creatives often experience time differently than analytical people. I think time is fascinating; it definitely feels fluid to me, the way it speeds up and slows down." Her perception of time is not unlike some of Einstein's dreams, where time is never a constant but changes in relation to other forces.

Kelly agrees, saying, "I feel very fortunate that I can actually lose time when I'm painting—it feels meditative, the creative process, and I'm not sure if this is something that other people feel in relationship to time. Maybe athletes? Just thinking about long distance runners here. . . ."

Notice how they talk wistfully about this sense of being outside time, kind of like the way people talk about flying in dreams, as if it's our natural state but one

we have trouble accessing. What is the appeal of losing track of time, of being lost in a world where time has no meaning and no power? For artists, it means that you can pursue an idea however far you need to go without having to rein yourself in, counting the minutes you're "wasting" in experiments and trials while keeping in the back of your mind that you have to make dinner and take your daughter to soccer practice. It's also the deeper pull of being able to slip out of this hour, this day, this year, and fall back into childhood, as Theo mentions, or even into another century. When Lisa immerses herself in research for a new figure, the centuries melt away.

For her, there is the definite sense that artists see time differently. She says, "My friends who are artists have no problem not hearing from me for years at a time. When we talk it is as if no time has passed. Friends and family who are not artists can be very hurt if I don't keep in touch with them regularly." For creative people, time unfolds differently, and the world of imagination often takes precedence over the world of facts and rules and, of course, time. Dreams and ideas are timeless—you've felt that, waking up from a dream that lasted for weeks only to have the clock insist that you'd slept for only half an hour. Remember how surreal that feels? If you're like me, you sometimes reach over and give the clock a little shake, just to make sure it's working.

As you begin to re-think your relationship with clock time, however, you're still arguing that you have to get things done on time, have to make deadlines and appear for appointments. "Sure, it's easy to adopt a *laissez-faire* attitude about time when you get to spend your days in the studio," you grumble. (Because *laissez-faire* is such an excellent word to use when you're grumbling.)

Full-time artists realize they have been given a luxury which others covet and crave. Lori admits, "I think of time as a precious resource, as valuable to those who don't have it as dollars to those who struggle financially. So in this scenario, I am lucky. I have the time to create. I respect it. I value it. I appreciate it. I try not to take it for granted."

Chris agrees: "I am fortunate to have a life in which I can focus on my creativity. Pretty much, my creativity comes first." Approaching time differently than most people is the key. It's not that you ignore responsibilities or shirk duties or any of those bad habits you've been taught to avoid since you first started school. Instead, it's a re-ordering of time by re-thinking what's important and giving what's important the time it deserves, while learning to spread that creativity onto everything else.

Carter says, "I certainly think I have a more creative relationship with time than most non-artists I know. I set my own schedule, I set my own goals, and I figure out how to fit it all in a day. That is one of the many beautiful things about being an artist: You call your own shots."

For Traci, who has given up her house temporarily because she's spending so much time traveling to teach workshops, time means little. "If I need to run errands or go to the gym, I can do so and work later in the day. If I have to travel to a workshop venue, I can do my work on the plane during my flight. There have been many days that I work until 4AM, which is a time most people would be sleeping. But since I set my own schedule, I can choose my working hours."

Rethinking what a daily schedule should look like is, admittedly, easier for someone who doesn't have a regular day job. But even if you do have to

A Witch's Bedtime Story—Theo Ellsworth

Time Flies—Susan Sorrell

Example from Judy Wise

"Whenever I have a task I'm dreading, I try to figure out how I can use it on my blog. Really, what a blog consists of is life presented in a creative way. So if I'm reluctant about all the work involved in making a cherry pie [*she says she uses this as an example because she would never actually make one*], I stage and photograph the process from start to finish and then weave what I hope will be a charming story around the event for my readers. That makes it fun for me and turns drudgery into art. By seeing the beautiful cherry pie through the eyes of my viewers, it becomes a summer icon of joy."

Traci Bautista

Chris Malone

Try This

Go back to the lists you made of all the creative and non-creative things you do throughout your days. What is the difference between the two? How does cooking dinner *differ from* sketching? *In both, you make something that wasn't there before. In both, you're creating something pleasant—at least in someone's opinion, depending on whether or not the dinner involves broccoli. Could it be that the main difference between the lists is mostly attitude? On the left you have "have to do" things, and on the right you have "get to do" things. How can you change the way you think about the have-to-do's?*

While it may be tough to keep the creative engine chugging throughout the work day, it's not impossible. I know this is true, because I once wrote a poem that went on to win a couple of awards and a nice check. I wrote it entirely during a string of workdays as a clerk at the Department of Animal Control. My work didn't suffer; the animals didn't get any less attention; and I was so much happier to be thinking about the lines of the poem than listening to the drama of my co-workers while I filed papers.

leave the house and go to work, there are still ways to make more creative use of the hours when you're not on the clock. Isn't that an apt way to think of work: being "on the clock"? Conversely, when you're not at work, you're "not on the clock." Start thinking about the rest of your day in those terms: *not being on the clock.* You'll have to keep appointments and do car-pool duty, but there are a lot of things that don't require a specific time frame. As you read about the ways our artists have made time work for them, think about how you could incorporate some of their techniques into your own life, whether it's your whole day as a working artist or just that chunk of it when you're truly "off the clock."

after years of having no new dreams, the same life day in and day out, I am suddenly alive again with ambition and goals. I am old enough to know that it is not the attainment that matters but rather the hope that the dream inspires.

I was going to tell you but then I changed my mind.

Mermaid—Judy Wise

Your Brain Loves Stories

Humans make up stories. We make up stories about things we don't understand, and we make up stories to help us remember what happens to us. We make up stories to console each other and to entertain ourselves when we gather around a fire. We are story-makers, and our brains thrive on creating them. There's no better way to keep your brain in gear than to make up stories about what's going on around you. The more imaginative and detailed, the happier your creative brain will be.

• Nothing gives your brain a more exciting workout than creating detailed stories from a single clue. Picture a woman with a tiny band-aid behind her ear. What happened? Did aliens implant a device there, so that she woke up this morning with a bandage she doesn't even know was there? Did a vampire bite her but miss her neck? Maybe it's a secret code tattooed there, and she's a spy.

• If you have a commute or car-pool duty, make up stories about the people in the cars next to you. Get your kids involved. Use the alphabet: The first person you see is an astronaut. Where is she going? That guy over there is a bareback rider. Why is he driving a moving van? And what about that clown disguised in regular clothes?

• If you teach, make up stories about the kids in your classes. You won't want to share these, but your stories can explain why Jeff is such a terror on Fridays and why Emily always wears green barrettes.

Your brain *loves* this kind of stuff. Give it stories, and it will give you ideas.

Rooster Sketches—Roz Stendahl

Going Off the Clock

One of the complaints that people have is the difficulty of the transition from the real world to that creative space inside their heads. One minute you're paying bills, and the next minute, you've walked into your studio and have switched to creative time. Only your brain is still in bill-paying mode, in work mode, left-brain mode, logical, clock-time mode. That switch from left brain to right brain, from day-to-day thinking to the place where inspiration comes from, is one of the things that consume way more time than we have to give. (Read more about this in Chapter 2.) The solution for many artists is that they have changed the way they think about their lives

Rather than make the distinction between "real life" and "time to create," they shift their focus. Real life becomes creative time. Everything they do is an expression of creativity.

Traci says, "Making time for creativity is important to me. Whether it's painting or creating a piece of artwork, taking photos throughout the day, cooking dinner, or designing for my product line—to the way I dress or the color of my hair—I make sure that it is involved in every aspect of my life." There's no division of day-to-day life, with "work" in one column and "creativity" in the other, with a constant juggling and shifting between the two.

Pam gets into her quilting studio after all the other work is done for the day. It would be easy for her to

Creativity at Work

Sure—you've got lots of things on your mind. But how you think about them can make all the difference between a long, draining day and hours that are an ongoing exercise in creativity, leaving you ready for that shift into studio mode.

• Carry a small notebook and sketch everything. Not elaborate drawings that take hours to complete, but thumbnail sketches of a co-worker's shoe or hand, or a dying plant in the foyer. If you don't want to sketch, make notes. If you have a job where your hands are constantly busy and you can't sketch or draw—if you're a stylist or working in manufacturing or farming or any of the jobs where you actually work with your hands—use your breaks. Instead of eating a candy bar, make a quick drawing. Sure, it's a little extra effort. But it's keeping your brain ready for the moment you leave work and go home and pick up the paintbrush.

• Make everything an adventure. Let your kids help you make a dinner where everything has to be orange. Or purple. One meal of eggplant and grape popsicles isn't going to hurt them. Remember the story about the people who had long sticks tied to their hands and couldn't eat until they realized they had to feed each other? Try that: Everyone at the table has to feed someone else. Take turns.

think of every day as being divided between non-creative tasks and those precious hours of creative studio time, but that's not the case. Pam doesn't look at all the chores as things that get in the way, but as creative challenges.

She says, "I try to make everything a creative project. That's how I fit it in. It just sort of seeps into everything I do. For example, recently I got tired of making 'to-do' lists, so I started making drawings and incorporating an abbreviated 'to-do' list into the drawing. It's made planning my day more fun—actually something I've started looking forward to each morning, instead of something I dread or avoid. I guess I operate on a *Mary Poppins* philosophy: 'Just a spoonful of sugar helps the medicine go down.' So I either figure out a way to make something creative and fun, or it doesn't get done."

Just that shift in thinking—from making a to-do list that's a left-brain chore of all the things that have to be accomplished before there's studio time, to making a to-do list that's a right-brain visual experiment for a project you're going to be working on later in the day—helps to create that sense of continuity and flow. In this way, writing down tasks is a chance to try out a new set of colored pencils or watercolors. You spend two minutes sketching a little cartoon of the guy at the quick-lube shop. It might sound like nothing, but it's that shift in thinking, that message to your brain about how you value creativity, plus the beginnings of learning how to engage your right brain in every task, that is vitally important. Keeping that part of your brain engaged makes everything else so much easier. Think of how much easier it is to sit down at your computer and fire off a quick e-mail if the computer is already up and running. It's the same way with your right brain: If it's already warmed up, there's no lag when you finally have a minute to get to the studio.

Roz says, "I don't really make time for creativity in my life; I just do the things I do, and they seem to all be labeled by society as creative." That doesn't mean that Roz never does any chores or tasks or "work." It means that, for her, the things she does are all imbued with that right-brain way of looking at even the most mundane job.

Lori says, "I tend to work between eight and twelve hours a day. It's hard for me to define a 'work day' because I mix in a lot of photography and Internet time, which are very recreational. Even though, technically, I am working, I enjoy these activities so much that it really doesn't seem like it should count as 'work hours.' My creativity doesn't begin and end in the studio. I try hard to infuse all aspects of my life with the same energy that goes into designing clothes and accessories."

Most of the artists in this book approach their lives that way—not necessarily by plan, but because it's the way they live. Their creativity comes first and they make everything else fit in.

Traci says, "Everything I do revolves around being an artist. I do what I love and have a passion for it, so it doesn't feel like work."

If you re-think your concept of time, you'll begin to see a spacious quality to your days that you would have sworn wasn't there yesterday. If you can imbue everything you do—from the client meetings to carpooling—with creativity, you'll find that the days feel more expansive, as if you've put a little bit of elastic in them. Being able to keep your brain up and humming is a first step toward having more time, and now we're ready for another step: learning to cultivate the flow between your left brain and your right brain.

Pam Says...

"Creativity is sort of like plumbing, I think, and if you've never had it installed in your house, it's pretty hard to get the water running there. But if you've gotten the plumbing installed (i.e., make your studio space for yourself, etc.) and maintain it, keep the pipes from freezing up in the winter and keep the sink from piling up with too many dirty dishes, pretty much you can turn it off and on through the day.

"And I try to turn it on as often as I can through the day (so that nothing gets too rusty) by interjecting creativity into anything I can."

Chapter 2

Making Time

Let's Face It: You Can't Do Everything

For most full-time artists, the business of art and the art itself often seem like two completely separate jobs, the quintessence of that left-brain, right-brain split. In this chapter, we're going to think about those two parts of our brains and about balance and flow, about being able to move back and forth between logical, business-like tasks and looser, more creative tasks and how this can help you transition from The Regular World into your time in the studio. We're going to take a really hard look at the things in our lives that are eating up the hours and keeping us from this flow. We've got a lot to think about, so let's start out with a couple of people who have more crammed into those hours than most of us even want to consider. If they can do it, though, you know there's hope for the rest of us.

Traci says, "Between creating artwork, traveling and teaching for two to three weeks a month, preparing for workshops, answering e-mail, sending out teaching proposals, updating all my Web properties, managing my online orders, writing articles and books, developing an Internet business and designing a product line, I work all hours of the morning and night. I probably work around eighty to one hundred hours a week." Just reading about it is enough to make you need to sit down with a cup of tea, isn't it? But she's not alone.

Tom, who was on the road about 230 days last year, knows exactly what it's like: "I am totally immersed in this

Carter Seibels

life of art and business. It's all I do all day, almost every day. I design, make, manage, plan and teach. Of course it isn't all of that every day, mind you; but the days are full with aspects of most of this. Multitasking is definitely taking place. When I'm back in New Orleans it only gets worse. My days at work are a kaleidoscope of activities. A flurry of e-mails, phone calls, meetings—big ones and little ones—trying to remember to eat lunch—then, finally, at around 5PM–6PM I can sit at the bench or stand at the drawing board and get to work on the 'work.'" Most of our artists are smiling ruefully at the to-do list for *every* day.

So how do they do it—get everything done and keep track of all their deadlines and commitments and still eek out a couple hours in the studio? If you take a look at a "typical" day for Traci, you'll wonder how she has time to do anything at all. Notice, however, how she manages to make time for all the good stuff.

What you'll notice here are the seamless transitions: On the plane, she's doodling and watching movies and working on projects. She talks to her family and downloads e-mail for work, flowing smoothly back and forth. It might seem exhausting to some of us, but to her it's

A Day in the Life of an Artist—Traci

Monday, in San Francisco for Mother's Day weekend with my family

12:30AM—finished packing suitcases and doing laundry for my trip

12:30AM–1:00AM—iChat with my friends before I leave

1:00AM–2:00AM—catch up on e-mails, work on workshop handouts, update workshop proposals

2:30AM–7:15AM—sleep

8:30AM–9:30AM—a little more catching up—print travel docs, sending out last-minute e-mails

10AM–11:30AM—breakfast at Mexico Tipico with my family; we're all flying out of SFO today

11:30AM–1:30PM—run to Michael's to buy a few supplies, trip to Kinko's to print handouts and info for my next book

1:30PM–3:15PM—travel time to SFO to drop off family for flights

3:15PM–4:15PM—catch up with friend over coffee at Starbucks

4:15PM–6:15PM—last minute travel details—pack carry-on, work on e-mails, follow-up phone calls to discuss upcoming workshops, editing photos for my blog, download camera photos to computer

6:45PM–7:45PM—dinner with girlfriends at Semo Sushi—yummy!

7:45PM–9:00PM—travel time to SFO, gas up rental car, return car and check in at International Terminal

9:00PM–10:40PM—on board before my flight takes off—call American Airlines to schedule travel from Sydney to Bali, call family, download my e-mail to work on it on the plane

10:40PM (Pacific Standard Time)—May 14, **6:00PM** (Australia Eastern Standard Time)—flight to Sydney—sleep most of my flight, make a list of to-do's, watch a couple movies, catch up on e-mail, work on interview questions, doodle in my journal, brainstorm and sketch project ideas

Dream Time

It may sound simplistic, but learning to make use of the time you spend dreaming can really boost your efforts to make all your time—waking and sleeping—into creative time. Dreams can inspire new pieces and, once you learn to use them, can be invaluable in helping solve design problems in on-going projects. Lisa gives an example:

"I find that I solve technical problems in my sleep. When you solve problems in dreams, there is a puzzle to the answer. Once you get past dream logic, the solution is obvious. I once redesigned the wire pelvis for my internal skeletons—it made it possible for me to do accurate and very realistic torsos, and that started me doing more nudes. In my dream, the parts of the pelvis were continents on an alien planet, which was water all the way down to a small central core. I was skipping along these big shapes until I realized that the shapes were what was important—they were the new wire designs."

Keep a notebook by the bed to record ideas. If dreaming interests you, look for books on lucid dreaming and working with your dreams.

Thomas Mann

energizing, and it allows her to do all the things she loves. If you can combine international travel with sketches for projects, surely there's a way to combine a day job with regular time in the studio.

In Chapter 3, we'll talk about the more structured ways of making time for everything. Here, let's consider the more organic approach that works best for some people. Instead of setting up a firm schedule, you allow yourself to flow from one task to the next, even if the tasks are widely divergent—say, bookkeeping and painting. I asked the artists about "right-brain" work versus "left-brain" work. Do they think of that kind of division?

Some, like Theo, are intimately aware of the different sides of their brain. He says, "I'm so right-brained that it's almost silly. I get easily lost and turned around when I leave the house. I ride my bike for blocks and blocks, only to realize that I've been going the wrong way. In order to be a responsible human being, I've tried to work all of my chores and responsibilities into the larger flow of my art.

The handwritten notes (left page):

for JAZZ FEST '06
Techno Techtone / Crab
Crawfish
Hurricane Pin Series   Redfish
Fleur De Lis Mirror   Frogs
Fridge Map Panel   Nutria

FOR LAKEFRONT
"THIS / SIDE PLANK MAN
x 18"   1" Alum_   Stone
                                 Fetish
                                 Plus
ODELS for SALE   NKS
Show   PA model system
MAKE MORE
MAKE Custom PEGBD
      Shelving
Pricing Your Work (Sculpture)

Notes—Thomas Mann

I try to picture the larger structure and shape of my life and keep everything in some kind of overall balance. I feel like I'm the captain of an invisible ship that I'm trying to keep afloat. Whenever I pull off a decidedly left-brained activity, I feel like it's quite a victory. Maneuvering through the world and trying to do things in the correct order at the correct time is challenging to me. I often feel like I don't naturally function the way one needs to function in order to get by in the world. I try to see it all as part of an elaborate art project." It's a fabulous idea—life as an art project—but as you can imagine, it's frustrating for artists like Theo to deal with left-brain tasks such as paperwork and taxes.

Solutions

Carry a voice-activated digital recorder in your pocket to record ideas when you don't have time to write them down. It's amazing how many things you can capture in spare moments throughout the day. Don't be intimidated by the sound of your own voice—you don't have to wax poetic here. Think of the shorthand you use to jot down notes in your notebook. Just hearing your voice saying "Red, like billboard on 3rd Street" may be everything you need to remind you of the entire idea. Recorders work when you can't write or draw, which is especially useful during that morning commute when the rest of us do *not* want you to reach for a pen.

For many of us, the secret is in learning how to make that smooth gear change that allows us to move from one activity to the next with no disruption. It's difficult to do this if you're not used to it, but it makes life so much simpler that it's worth the effort to practice. It all goes back to what we discussed in Chapter 1, about keeping the creative part of your brain engaged and ready to go.

Lori says, "That is the joy of this creative life—to be able to move from one thing to another and try to keep it balanced. I tend to go with my gut—if I want to spend a couple hours photographing my work, I do that. When I'm in the mood for a specific activity, I put all of my energy into it and am usually happy with the result. The same goes for inputting receipts into QuickBooks, designing a new shoulder bag, or going to the grocery store—all of it brings me joy and satisfies a different dimension of my life. When I'm in the studio, I can get lost in the right-brain

Sometimes—Kelly Rae Roberts

'zone' with no recognition of time or what's happening around me. But many times those right- and left-brains intersect, and I find myself 'zoned' in the more logical processes of the left brain," she says. "I guess what I'm trying to say is that both sides of my brain bring me great joy."

Chris, a man with a very healthy attitude toward time, says, "I let time present itself, and I deal with it. I try to keep a balance in my life between my art and other things that are important to me, which is sometimes difficult."

That balance becomes easier when the lines between kinds of tasks blur. Carter has been working a lot on achieving balance, and she says, "Sometimes I'll be making beads, and suddenly I remember something that I need to do on the computer. So I stop making beads and do it. I'm flexible with my time, as long as I get everything done."

Pam says simply, "My days pretty much all blend together, or you might say, 'get all mixed up.'" Because she's working with her sculptor husband on parts of various projects, she has to be able to move back and forth easily depending on what part of a project needs attention at any

Teesha Moore

Take a Hard Look

You're going to have to take a hard look at how
you spend your time, and the way to do that is to
keep track of every minute. Do this for a week,
and you can see where the big time-eaters lie in
wait. If you're running errands every afternoon
on the way home from work, you're spending an
hour or more that you could have spent in the
studio. It may seem that you have to do all this
running around, but you don't. Consolidate the
errands into one afternoon. The rest of the week,
head straight home. Once you get home, go
straight to your studio, ignoring everything else,
because this is Free Time. It's time you would
have been running to the dry cleaners or the post
office and wouldn't have been home, anyway.
Pretend you're playing hooky from life. Drop
your bag by the door, kick off your shoes, put on
your studio apron and get busy. A tiny glass of
wine might be nice.

31

particular time. "It varies, since I have several different
types of roles to play; I have to be flexible." She mentions
that she even works in her sleep, allowing the flow to
continue into her subconscious. Check out Lisa's story
(*Dream Time*, page 28) about how dreams contribute
solid, logical information in their own private language.

Carter says, "In my mind, there's not really much of a
division between the business side and the creative side.
Whatever I'm working on, unless it's a really mundane
task like tax preparation, I tend to get into the flow of it,
and that's what makes it work. As far as all the other 'life'

Artist with Children

Having children, especially young children, presents a whole 'nother set of time challenges. Judy Wise says, "When I lecture, I make a joke about artists not having children. One only has so many hours in a lifetime." But for all those artists who have children and have gotten sort of attached to them, there's still the importance of finding time to work. It requires discipline: You have to discipline yourself to discipline your children so that they don't grow up thinking it's your job to entertain them every waking moment. She adds, "To be honest, when my princesses were little, I hired sitters a lot to allow me to attend art school. The desire to create art and draw and learn was an overwhelming passion with me when I was young. I look back in guilt now, but my daughters are my best friends and assure me that it was all right."

Judy Perez, whose two are at home with her all day—and are now teenagers—has some excellent time-making suggestions.

"When my daughter was an infant, I used to roll her up in a receiving blanket and lay her on her side; and I found that I could open large books of art with beautiful graphic images and stand one up next to her. She would gaze at the images for a minute or two, then make a little noise; and I would turn the page, and she would quiet again, gazing at the next page for a few minutes. This would go on for almost half an hour. I could get quite a bit done this way. She always had a great attention span growing up. She is now an amazing artist, and I think this foundation of visual imagery may have had something to do with it."

32

Traci Bautista

She adds these tips:

• "I never spent precious nap time cleaning the house because that was ideal, uninterrupted creative time."

• "It helps to have kids get used to the idea from the beginning that there will be part of the day devoted to making art. I would often set my kids up with a project of their own while I was working. Sometimes it would be related to what I was doing; sometimes it would be their own project."

• "If you live in a neighborhood with other children, sometimes you can employ a mother's helper for a few hours. Basically this is a kid who is too young to babysit on their own but can do a good job of keeping the kids involved and playing while you work."

tasks, I have learned to find peace in the motion that I go through, so things like vacuuming and doing the laundry are more of a down time for me. I have always liked to clean and run errands, so I remind myself to continue to find the joy in these activities. The way I see it, it's all in how you look at it."

The "everything else" in your life—the day job, the childcare, the household chores, lawn work and shopping—doesn't have to be an interruption or an imposition. As you train your brain to spend more time in its creative mode, you'll find ways to encourage creative thinking, no matter what you're doing.

Susan says, "My time just melts together. I don't have

Jessica and Chelsea—Lisa Lichtenfels

Setting Studio Boundaries

- If your studio has a door you can shut, do that. Get one of the signs shopkeepers use with a clock face and "Will return at:" and use it to let people know when you'll be available.

- If you must have a phone in your studio, turn off the ringer. Use your answering machine to screen calls and collect messages. If you're worried about missing an important message, make it a habit to check each time you get up to take a bathroom break or get another cup of tea.

- Let your friends and family know what hours you can't be interrupted. It's difficult to stick to it at first, but if you consistently say, "I'm sorry, I'm working," they'll get used to the idea. The trick here is not to give in and say, "Oh, OK—I'll go for coffee just this one time."

normal hours and don't work just five days a week. My life is art, 24/7. It is a passion and not just my business. So the marketing and making of art go hand in hand for me, and there is no definite line between them."

Teesha tells of her struggles with this very issue, saying, "About four years ago, I moved my office into a spare bedroom and out of my studio space because every time I was working in the studio, I would feel guilty about all the paperwork that needed to get done. Four years later I moved it back into my studio in an attempt to re-integrate the paperwork and business side of things into my art. Before moving it back, I found that having the office in its own little room encouraged me to spend an inordinate

Moon Garden—Judy Coates Perez

amount of time doing 'business' and not enough time making art. I love having the two together again."

So. You begin to establish some sort of flow, moving smoothly from one task to another. You finally manage to get a couple of sweet hours in the studio, time when you can work on your current project. And then: the interruptions. The phone rings. Your best friend drops by and wants to take you to lunch. Your partner comes in and asks where you put the hammer. It's enough to make you give up and turn your studio into a storage room. How can you establish a flow if things keep jamming up the stream?

Judy Wise says she likes to try to divide her days, with "mornings for business and afternoons for art, but that is only a loose template. In actuality, the phone

Moth Eaten—Pam RuBert

Take Advantage of Shortcuts

Carter says, "I find shortcuts where I can. For instance, Trader Joe's has great meal-helpers, such as already-cooked lentils and already-cooked beets. And lentils are much better for me than potato chips!"

Other suggestions from artists:
• Avoid shopping—try to buy online or by mail order so you don't have to go to the mall.

• Find out if your grocery store and pharmacy will deliver.

• Combine doctor and vet appointments and all the errands you can't do by e-mail, phone or Internet into one or, at most, two days a month. This keeps you from having to run all over town several times a week.

• Check around to see if you can afford a cleaning service once a month. Knowing that someone is coming to do the big chores will keep you from having to think about them.

Lisa's Story

Lisa employs her husband, Jerry, who is a poet. He does the things she no longer has time for; but, in the beginning, it took a lot of adjusting:

"When Jerry and I first got married, I tried to be the domestic one. Jerry and I have different levels of cleanliness. I found that I was spending all day cleaning—I would get the place nice, and within like ten seconds, Jerry would mess it up. Basically, I was becoming a housewife, not an artist. We had a terrible argument about it, and I said, 'Well, if you want to live in this mess, so be it. I will slum, too!'

"I didn't think I would be able to take it, but who cares? I had my life back, and the art made up for everything and more. Now the whole house is 'Jerry-world' except for my studio. My studio has to be clean, and I put my foot down there.

"Since living this way, I have given up many friends and a good bit of family. It is amazing how many people judge you on your house. A certain relative came by just once and has been cool and distant since. The last time we met, it was carefully arranged to be at a restaurant in town. Of course some people get it. The last photographer who visited wants to come back and take photographs not of me or my sculpture, but of Jerry's kitchen. Really, it is a tightly crammed work of Bohemian eclectic décor that would put any bower bird to shame. When I first met Jerry I was fascinated by the apartment he had fashioned above his parents' garage. I didn't know it then, but I was in love with his capacity to nest."

rings, people drop in, emergencies arise. When you work at home, where my studio is, you get used to constant interruptions and interference. I do my best to flow with it and not get into a twist. It's easier in the long run. As an old hippie, I often repeat to myself the old adage 'roll with the flow.' It doesn't help to be rigid; you have to develop some bend, or you'll end up throwing dishes and furniture. Ask me how I know."

Roz agrees, noting, "I also try not to be rigid. Things happen to disrupt your routine—a dog or family member becomes ill, a client changes an appointment. I've tried to find ways to adapt to those needs by shifting things in my schedule. I figure, for instance, when a friend interrupts me, I need to stop and really listen to that friend because that really is my life and his life and I want to be present for that. I know, from past experience, that I can just jump right back into my work, because that's how I've trained myself. But for that moment when he needs to talk to me, I want to be present and not worry about how I'm going to get something done. I try to constantly practice patience to myself, and flexibility. I hope to get it right just about the time I die. But I know I'm getting better at it."

It's an excellent attitude, indeed. But not all of us can deal with interruptions. For some of us, they're deadly. They not only break your focus, but they're irritating. You have proof, once again, that no one values your time as an artist. (For more on staying focused, check out Chapter 6.) You have to learn how your brain works and figure out whether you can tolerate interruptions or not. If not, you need to do everything in your power to minimize them.

Lisa keeps her mornings sacrosanct for the most creative work, when she isn't to be disturbed at all. For the rest of day, she says, it "flows back and forth" between artwork and organizational details. "I try to keep my life simple, but business things demand some time. I never do them in the morning, and I try to break up these chores into small tasks between the real work. Being a somewhat odd person, I don't have many friends; although the ones I do have are priceless. They tend to live far away,

Try This

What are the things you have to do in a day? List them all, no matter how insignificant they seem. Then go through and highlight the things that only you can do. That would include things like "brush teeth," of course, but also important things like "paint." Do not include things like "mow the lawn" and "make the beds"—look at those things and divide them into two groups: things someone else can do (mow the lawn) and things that don't really have to be done (make the bed). Who else might mow the lawn? Other people who live in the house with you, or a neighborhood kid who wants to make a few bucks, or a lawn service? Or what about giving up the lawn, saving the money you would spend on watering for a year, and hiring someone to help you start xeriscaping? As for the beds: toss on some extra pillows and go for that careless, rumpled look. A lot of routine maintenance is really about the standards we've imposed on ourselves. Read what Lisa has to say about that in Lisa's Story, page 36.

so I keep in touch by e-mail or phone." Keeping in touch with friends by e-mail—even when they live right across the street—allows you to respond when you're not in the middle of something. You can schedule a coffee break by e-mail without ever having to interrupt the flow of your morning. This works perfectly for someone who needs not to be interrupted by drop-in visitors and enticing invita-

tions. If you need solitary creative time for work but find yourself constantly interrupted in the studio by well-meaning friends and family who crave just a few minutes to chat, maybe it's time to set some boundaries.

While it may seem harsh, there's a stark truth to integrating creative time into your real life. While it's wonderful to imagine a life where you have a successful career in international banking and unlimited time in the studio and

Roz's Story

"I had a car accident in 1996 and really injured my neck. It took a long time to recover and get back to work. I found that while I liked things neat and tidy, I had to make a choice: make things neat and tidy, or get my work done. I couldn't do both. Because of that I looked at my options and found that if I gave up my ice cream consumption (which was substantial per month [*Author's note: This is amazing, as Roz is a very small person*]), I could afford to have a cleaning service come in every other week and do all the things I could no longer easily do because of my injuries. This was a revelation for me. It made perfect sense to use my productive time at the computer or the drawing table and do those things which only I could do, and for which I get paid, and then pay other folks to do those things I could no longer do. I ended up with no frustration, more money because I actually worked more (not being exhausted from trying to clean with the limitations I faced); I healed more quickly, and I ended up with better eating habits."

37

a rich and varied social life and hours with your family and friends and time to relax and unwind and travel and go to movies and lie on the beach, something's got to give, and something has to go. You've heard it before, and you know it's true: You can't have everything. No one can. Sacrifices have to be made here, just as they do with other areas in life. I'm sorry to have to tell you this, but, to make more time for creativity, you're going to have to jettison the things you can live without and prioritize the rest.

So what kinds of things have to go? It all depends on you, of course—what you need and what you can live without. I would have thought, given my personal aversion to television, that it would be one of the first things artists would jettison. I was very, very wrong. Many are avid—although discriminating—TV viewers.

Pam says, "I can get a lot of drawing done in the

Taming the Internet

The Internet is truly a wonderful thing. For working artists who don't get out much and don't have extensive contact with other artists, it can be a life saver. But we all know it can also eat up hours like they were candy. Remember what we talked about earlier, about how having time for everything is impossible? Well, it's equally impossible to know every bit of information, to stay informed about everything that happens and every trend. You have to be selective and figure out what's really important for you. Looking at other people's art and reading about it on the Web is fun, but is it really any substitute for the time you could be putting in in your studio? Roz offers the following advice for curbing the habit.

- "If possible, have your computer in a room away from your studio so you won't be tempted to 'check just this one thing.' If you need to look something up, write it down and do it all at once later in the day."

- "Set aside a specific time of day to do all your online connecting. Save everything for that

block of time—don't say, 'Oh, I'll just check out this blog.' Make a note and make it wait."

- "Set a timer for however long you'd like to allow yourself to surf. Be firm: When the timer goes off, get up and move away from the computer."

- "Share Internet time with the rest of the family. If your daughter is standing behind you whining that it's her turn, you'll be less likely to get lost in linksville."

- "Weed out the things you don't really love. If you're mindlessly clicking on links, you're running into a lot of things that really don't interest you all that much. Limit yourself to half a dozen blogs, or designate one day a week when you'll devote one hour to reading blogs. (And if you're going, 'An hour? That's not nearly enough!' then you know it's time to crack down.)"

- "Make the distinction between studio time and computer time. Your time in the studio is for art; set some other, completely separate time for the computer and think of them as two discrete activities."

evening at home watching comedies or movies."

Judy Perez says, "I do not watch a lot of TV, but I have my favorite shows that have become kind of ritualistic. Sunday I love to wake up and watch the political talk shows and knit, sipping tea before anyone else wakes up. This recharges my batteries for the week ahead. I often sit down late in the evening and watch political satire shows with my kids while working on some kind of handwork. Both my kids have picked up this habit as well, with my daughter drawing and my son folding paper while any TV is being watched."

Roz says, "I enjoy TV and watch a lot of it, typically beading or weaving at the same time. I read *The Wall Street Journal* but not the local paper. I have friends who tell me about local news and events. I think I return the favor by telling them other things of interest."

Chris says, "I certainly keep up with current events through television, newspaper and magazines," and Lori Marsha Sandstedt adds, "I love popular culture and am intrigued by television, movies and magazines. I'm a sucker for red-carpet award shows. I love going to the

Chris Malone

News by E-Mail

On the other hand, the computer can help you save time. When I quit listening to the news and reading the newspaper, I signed up for breaking news online from *The New York Times* and *The Washington Post*. It's free, and I find out about the big stories without having to wade through the sensationalist nonsense that fills most newspapers. There are always links I can follow if I want to find out more, but usually the headlines are enough.

movies and am drawn in as much by the fashion as the plot and character development."

Lisa watches television even in her studio, explaining, "Seventeen years ago I was told I was developing eye problems doing too much close work. The doctor told me to look out the window regularly, but I soon got tired of the same view. So I measured the distance I need to look away and placed a TV there. Every so often I glance up, and it has saved my eyesight. The harder the task, the less interesting the TV shows I play. I find I can do really difficult work when a bad sci-fi movie is on. When I draw I need total silence. Since getting cable, I am very happy with TV; there are a lot of really good programs. I also

Art Desk—Pam RuBert

buy college courses on DVD. Right now I am studying the Renaissance."

So what do they give up—what things do they avoid that ensnare the rest of us?

Judy Wise says, "Are there things I've given up? Well, let's just say that normal people have furniture, clothes, material things that I've chosen not to mess with. I was in therapy nearly two years sorting out what was important to me in my life. I discovered that what made me happy was not what the culture told me would make me happy. I feel nicely adjusted now, and it makes all the difference."

As you listen to working artists, you find that this sort of adjustment—in the way they live, but also in the way they think about the way they live—is at the core of their relationship with time and creativity. For them, the things much of society values—the nice car, the 401K, the new furniture—are less important than living a creative life.

Theo is very careful about how he spends his time, explaining, "I see time as a precious and slippery thing. It's easy to fill up your time with things that, by the end of the day, haven't really advanced or fulfilled you as a person. I find myself wanting to sidestep most mass media and

pop culture and stick to what's vital and personal to me. I haven't watched TV for years and years. I like reading books. I like movies, but I try to be selective. A bad movie, to me, is a couple of hours of my life I will never get back."

Maybe it doesn't surprise you to hear that, for many artists, the biggest time-sucker they have to avoid is—*ta da!*—the Internet. Oh, the Internet! As much as we love it, with its entertaining blogs and fabulous Web sites full of eye candy and the immediacy of e-mail, we hate it, too. Artists bemoan the hours lost in surfing blogs and clicking on links to other blogs and yet more blogs and then a Web site that leads them to another Web site and, well . . . It isn't just in the studio that many of them find themselves looking up and realizing a couple of hours have slipped away unnoticed.

Kelly explains, "The minute I get online, I lose efficiency in my work day. Although I love—and am very committed to—reading my favorite blogs and checking in on my favorite Flickr groups, I tend to get sucked into the vortex of the Web; and before I know it, hours have gone by. I try hard to avoid the Internet during working hours, unless it's work-related, of course."

Lori says, "My biggest time zapper is the Internet. One Web site links to another, a Flickr leads to a Google, which leads to a blog. Before I know it, it's 10AM and I'm still in my pajamas and holding onto a cold cup of coffee. So I tend to reserve those activities for late at night after everyone else has gone to bed."

Roz says, "Overall, I think of myself as a media slut. Things could only be worse if I liked the Internet. As it is, being a print person, I haven't really warmed up to the Internet and don't spend much time on it." Roz offers her own solutions, in *Taming the Internet* on page 38.

Judy Perez says, "I often don't differentiate working time and making art from regular life. I would have a hard time not making art, so I never think about making time for it. What I have to make time for is cleaning the house, getting exercise, paying the bills . . . I think what I do differently from others is not keeping an immaculate house."

You can have both—see *Roz's Story* on page 37—but it's tough. What's easier is readjusting the way you think.

What are you willing to change to make more time for your art? Is it really important to vacuum every week? What about meetings and groups you belong to?

There are things you're going to have to give up to have time for creativity. Big things, little things, all kinds of things—only you know what they are. But to the artist, all those things are secondary anyway.

Theo says, "I've heard someone say that the only way to make a living at art is to be proficient only at art. I don't know how true that is, but it does feel like the only thing I'm really good for. I don't really have a problem with making time for art; I actually have the opposite challenge. My girlfriend is always challenging me to put down my pen and take a break, get out of the house, go on a walk. I

Dreamer—Judy Wise

feel like I've made a lot of choices over the years to put art first in my life."

In the end, you begin to see that that's what it's all about: choices. You choose what's important and where you want to put your energy because only you can figure out what you can live with and what you can live without. Once you've done that, you might want to build a little structure into your days so that the spare hours have room to make an appearance. If your brain works best on a schedule, then Chapter 3 is going to make you very, very happy.

41

Chapter 3

Corralling Time

Sometimes You Need a Whip and Spurs

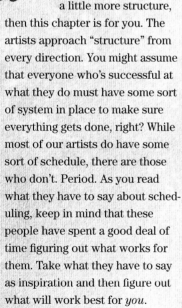

If your creative brain is one that needs just a little more structure, then this chapter is for you. The artists approach "structure" from every direction. You might assume that everyone who's successful at what they do must have some sort of system in place to make sure everything gets done, right? While most of our artists do have some sort of schedule, there are those who don't. Period. As you read what they have to say about scheduling, keep in mind that these people have spent a good deal of time figuring out what works for them. Take what they have to say as inspiration and then figure out what will work best for *you*.

First, the non-schedulers. Chris says, "I do not follow a schedule; I just let creativity happen." He manages to get everything done, but he lets it occur organically, in a balanced flow of life in his home and garden. Lori agrees: "Ha! A schedule? Hardly. I am more comfortable just getting into the zone and working on something for

June's Kitchen—Roz Stendahl

as long as I think I need to."

Judy Wise says, "I like to get into a daily groove if I can, but I am not a machine. I am very gentle with myself, very forgiving at this stage of life. When I was younger I was much more disciplined, but then I realized that was killing the joy for me. Now I seduce the muse; I don't put pressure on her. It works much better for me."

Tom's Schedule

Tom's summer schedule might look like this:
"I'll be traveling to Anderson Ranch in Steamboat Springs, Colorado, to teach a five-day workshop on model making for sculptors, then immediately fly to Allentown, Pennsylvania, to teach a Design for Survival workshop for the Pennsylvania Goldsmiths' Guild, then immediately fly to Seattle where I'll have to build a display for my booth at the Bellevue Festival of the Arts, then drive it down the coast to San Francisco and set it up for the American Craft Council Show at Fort Mason. So I have to plan where, when and how all of the equipment necessary for these very different events gets shipped and delivered."

Carter Seibels

43

Lisa mentions that she has moved away from a time in her life when she imposed a very rigid schedule on herself, explaining, "Several years ago when I had a difficult deadline for a major museum exhibit, I made myself get up at 6AM. For two and a half years I worked that way to make the deadlines, but I paid for it with back problems and other health issues. Now I get up when I feel like getting up and start the day without that pressure."

Carter says, "Oh, if only I could be as structured as I think I am! I'm one of those people who get a gazillion things done in a day, but at all hours of the day, in no particular order every day. And I'm all over the place while I'm getting things done. When I was first out of college, I tried to set this schedule for myself where I was up at 6AM, walked my dog Finn, showered, out the door to Starbucks, and working in my garage studio by 9AM.

Carter's Schedule

"Currently I am up pretty early, and I head to either a 6AM or 7:45AM Bickram Yoga class, come home and shower, quick walk with Finn, then off to the office. Some days I'm there at 9:30AM; some days I'm there by noon. But what matters more to me now is how much I get done in a day. I tend to get a second wind at night, so oftentimes I will make beads at night or do computer work at night. I love to get in bed and work on the computer and do things like research new supplies."

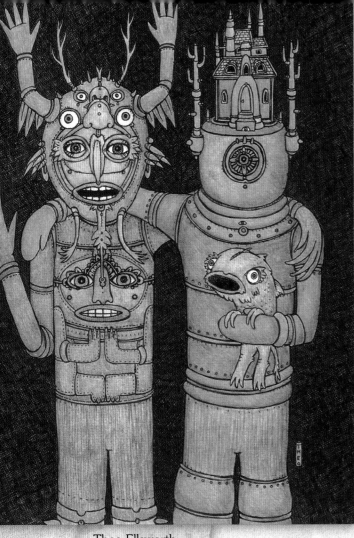

Theo Ellsworth

'To-Do List' that covers a week or a month of the next big tasks on my list. That way I can focus on the bigger picture, rather than what I need to be doing in the next thirty minutes."

Even the artists who don't have a set schedule usually have a way of keeping track of what needs to be done during the course of a day. Susan relies on calendars: "I keep several calendars that I can see from any vantage point in my studio, and I keep lists! I learned that in college from my roommate, Carol. I learned in graduate school to have a plan and to start early on what you need to do."

Traci says, "To keep up with my ever-changing, hectic schedule, I use a couple different methods to keep track of everything. I have a calendar/notebook to keep track of workshops and to-do lists. I have another calendar in Entourage that syncs with my iPhone on all the events going on for the month."

Theo's Schedule

"Most days, I just get up and get working. I'll make a quick breakfast and make tea, and sit down at my drawing table. Some days I hardly move from there, and then it's suddenly evening. One day a week I work at the art gallery that I'm a member of. On weekends I usually set up and sell my work at an outdoor art market in downtown Portland. Some days, I work over at a friend's studio, for company. I think it's good to switch things up a lot, stay active, keep things fresh. I'm not someone that likes to have too rigid a routine, but I have a strong need to always keep working, yet not lose touch with the outside world or a sense of community."

It worked pretty well, but it got really boring really fast. I've tried implementing all sorts of schedules for myself over the years, and I think it's safe to say that whatever the schedule is, it'll change in a few months. I have learned that when I try to impose a rigorous schedule on myself, sticking to the schedule stresses me out because when things come up spontaneously, then I freak out because they're not 'in my book.' I have learned that it's much more effective for me to have a more open-ended

Tom, who's on the road almost as much as Traci, prefers a less high-tech method. He says, "I keep a little Rhodia pad in my back pocket and that is where every idea in the form of a drawing or a thought goes down as a reference to jump-start the creative process back in the studio. Lists are the only way I can keep it all lined up in my head—lists, lists and more lists. Lists for me, lists for my staff. Lists on paper, on white boards, on the notepad on the dash of the van, in my back-pocket Rhodia pad. Sometimes the writing of the lists is merely a formality because the act of doing so plants it nicely in the list reservoir in my brain. I have so little creative time in the studio I have to be very focused and productive. No

Remember—Kelly Rae Roberts

Kelly's Schedule

"For me, it's definitely helpful to keep a schedule and at least try to stick to it. My perfect workday would go like this—this is the schedule I try to keep Monday–Saturday. Sundays are free.

9AM—wake up and eat breakfast
9:45–11AM—exercise/stretch (MWF)
9:45–11AM—run errands/chores (T/Th)
11–noon—shower and lunch
Noon–4PM—work
4–4:30PM—snack break and walk my doggie
4:30–8:30PM—work
8:30–midnight—read, spend time with my husband, etc.
Midnight—bedtime

"I try hard to keep a schedule that reflects both studio hours and regular-life hours. I really, really thrive on balance. My creativity needs that, too."

foolin' around—well, not much, anyway. I don't have the luxury of 'putzing-around' time, which I have so treasured over the course of this career and which, in the past, was necessary to launching the seriously productive times. I have to hit the ground running now in order to keep the production of the one-of-a-kind work that is selling better than ever in my career."

Even though Theo doesn't like a lot of structure, the deadlines and shows require some way of keeping track of things. He explains, "When I have a lot of things to juggle, I'll end up making lists and putting them in the order that they need to get done. If there's something that I need to do at a certain time, I'll sometimes set the alarm on my phone. This allows me to completely get engrossed in my work and lose track of time for a while. Then the alarm reminds me to come back into the world and head out the door. I feel like I'm barely pulling off some kind of complicated, circus-juggling act a lot of days. I like to feel like I'm on top of things and a little

Sometimes I get a routine going. . . but nothing like that ever seems to really stick for long, and I am constantly tinkering with my schedule. I've learned not to beat myself up when I can't do everything I think I should and also to not be afraid to break the routine and take advantage of the really beautiful and exciting opportunities that the

Teesha's Schedule

"I do try to have a structure in that I start my day with coffee around 6:30AM. I use the time driving down to get it as a time of meditation. I thank the heavenly beings that help me get through life, I thank the cells in my body for keeping me well, and I am present for the trees that line the road. I spend some time chatting with the baristas and always thank them for what they do. As I drive home, I thank the coffee for how good it tastes, I state my intention that this day will be a great day for new ideas and getting things done and making me fulfilled. I take a half hour to straighten the house and make some breakfast before heading to the studio around 8AM. I usually have a list of things that need my immediate attention, and this is what I work on. Some things just keep getting pushed month to month as more urgent things take place. Unfortunately, it's the things that get pushed that give me the most excitement—my crazy ideas I want to try.

"I use the time between 4PM and 6PM to exercise or walk the dog or read or cook. Then after dinner, between 7PM and 10PM, is when I do the fun stuff."

Journal—Teesha Moore

ahead of the game; but I rarely feel this way. I just try and roll with it and do the best that I can."

And even though Lisa gave up the rigid out-of-bed-by-6AM schedule she once kept, she still likes to have her days well organized. She says, "I do have a time structure in my studio. It starts with a list, usually twenty items, although I rarely do all of them. In the morning, I start with the most pressing creative project and do what is necessary to make headway on that. After lunch, I check off the things I got done in the morning and put numbers to the rest of the day's action items. The afternoon is more structured, and I do business, aerobics, e-mails—whatever needs to be done between creative tasks."

Pam says, "I always want to be one of those people who has some sort of regular routine for creativity but somehow can never get my life to fit into that shoe box.

friends. She says, "I know I have my mornings and late evenings to catch up on household chores, get to the grocery store, have dinners with friends and family, pay bills, return calls unrelated to art business. I also try hard to keep Sundays totally free so that I have one day a week to just rest and regroup for the week. When I abandon

Journal Page—Judy Wise

world presents to me. Because my schedule is always changing, I think I've developed the ability to pretty much be creative at the drop of a hat, because any time I get a free hour or day or week, I want to take advantage of it. I keep a master list of projects that are current and for each try to list at least the next actionable step. Over the years I've kind of developed an inner sense that tells me what needs to be done, and how much time I have left to do it."

For Kelly, having a firm schedule provides the balance she needs to be creative (see *Kelly's Schedule*, page 45 and *Kelly's Method*, page 50). Before she learned to schedule her time, she found she was working constantly and never making time for rest or getting together with

Pam's Schedule

"I used to keep a notebook organizer; now I use a calendar on my laptop, but in both cases I record important deadlines and what I have done, not by the minute, but by the hour. Sometimes my calendar ends up with big holes when I've gotten lazy or forgotten, but in general I try to fill in rough blocks of time—I used to use highlighters on the paper calendar; now I use the computer settings—to color code art activities (red) as opposed to business (blue) as opposed to personal (green—which can also mean Waste of Time because that's where shopping and watching TV fall, but also important stuff like time spent with family and friends).

"The reason for recording and color coding is that it's hard to plan how you're going to spend your time if you aren't really honest or don't know how you tend to spend your time. I like to look back at a week and see a nice balance of red, blue and green because I feel it is important to have balance in one's life, and a balanced one will be more productive and better in the long run for everyone involved—also happier and healthier."

the schedule is when I start to feel overwhelmed: The bills pile up, the laundry piles up, the dishes need to get done. Sometimes I really want to rebel against keeping a schedule, but I've learned that keeping one actually gives me a bit more freedom in the long run."

Teesha says, "I find that it is easier to devote entire days to a particular project or task [*Author note: see Teesha's Schedule, page 46*]. When I try to do just a little of each thing per day, I am constantly having to switch gears; and the work never seems to have a chance to really get going. So, for instance, I devote Mondays to working on my magazine, Tuesdays are reserved for dealing with all things related to the retreats I plan, Wednesdays I deal with everything having to do with Zettiology and my Web site, and Thursdays are devoted to making stuff. Fridays are usually days in which Tracy and I go into Seattle to explore, journal at coffee shops, check out galleries and eat at some new restaurant. We find a day like this really jazzes us up with new ideas and

Challenges

Sometimes goals can be too easy, the same-old-same-old kind of thing we've been doing forever. Sometimes we need to shake things up and challenge ourselves.

Lori says, "My overriding goal is to continue to do things that challenge me. I want to feel uncomfortable. I want to do something that scares me a little. I want to say 'yes' when my first reaction is to say 'no.'" What things are you scared to try? Make a list and then pick one and put it on your list of goals.

Caotrin—Lori Sandstedt

a breath of fresh air. Saturdays are reserved for working on the house and yard, and then Sundays are free days—we can do nothing or we can make art or we can work or whatever we feel like doing. In the in-between times during the day (an hour in the morning before I 'go to work,' an hour I take for lunch, a couple of hours between 4PM and 6PM, etc.) I squeeze in answering

Lori Sandstedt

Meeting Deadlines

Recently, Carter was preparing for both a wholesale show for her bead company and making necklaces to go in Hollywood Gifts Bags at an event that benefited Camp Ronald McDonald. She kept notes to explain how she managed to get it all done:

"I have made two lists: One is a list of all the pieces of jewelry that I need to make. The second is a list of all of the things that I need to do to get ready for these two events. On my jewelry list, I have made color-coded symbols for myself of which pieces I've made the beads for, which ones I've strung, which ones I need to photograph, and which ones are going where. And I mark things off as I go. I have calculated the number of days that I have to get all of this done (ten) and the number of pieces that I need to make each day to get it all done. So far I'm right on track, maybe a bit ahead of the game—pretty unusual! Because I have created this system, it's easy to see how I'm doing in terms of meeting my deadlines."

e-mails, doing a load of wash, running to the post office, getting groceries, cleaning the house, reading, etc. I mostly do my journaling and art making in the evenings, either while listening to music or watching TV. I've been watching less and less TV, as it just seems to distract me too much."

The key to scheduling creative time is knowing what time of day you feel most creative. If you have a day job, you're obviously going to have to work around that; but it still helps to know whether you feel more creative early in the morning or late at night. Our circadian rhythms differ, and what works for one person will feel counterintuitive to someone else. Lisa knows that she does her best, most creative work in the morning, so that's when she does those tasks, putting off the other things—the simpler handwork, the business tasks—until later in the day. Roz also makes use of the morning hours for more intense tasks. She says, "I use my most productive hours, which are morning hours, that first burst of energy and attention when I sit down in the morning, to work on the most creative tasks I have to get through. Lately I've also

Journal—Roz Stendahl

The Bundle
is back

july 3. 2008

Today at about 2 p.m. I went out on the new bike for 47 mins. That's what it took to get from home to St. Clair and back on the River Rd Parkway. The moment I unbraided my hair and put it back in a pony tail I knew it was a power pony tail. I already felt the urge to go fast. I was transported back to college and wanting to peddle, enjoying peddling, the exhuberance, the rush. Today I couldn't even get the gear changes down right (and my former bike was better than this one - but this one is great for me now - for where I am now, no longer having asperations of whizzing past folk). Yet despite still learning the gears I had great passages of speed and rhythm and ease and effort. And I peddled with a crazy smile on my face, enjoying every second.

Kelly's Method

"I absolutely keep short and long term goals to help stay on track. I have a system where I write down my monthly goals and then plug in actual 'to-do's' for each of those goals, into my weekly schedule. So, for example, if my long-term goal this month is to submit to two magazines, then I'll put on my to-do list for Week One something like, 'Research submission opportunities for 2 magazines.' Then the next week I'll put on my to-do list 'Gather material and send in submissions for XYZ magazine,' and so on. I do the same with art making. If my long-term goal is to have twenty finished paintings in two months, then I specifically write what that means for each week on those two months, whether it means painting two or three pieces per week. Once I have my long-term goals dissected into weekly to-do's, then I can further break that down into daily to-do's. This little system helps me not only to make goals, but also, to actually stay on track and accomplish them. Of course, some months and weeks are better than others, but having it written down into tangible steps is really helpful for someone like me who thrives on task-mastering."

had to use that time for detail work on paintings because I find that my eyes might be too tired at the end of the day. But the detail work is very creative, so it isn't really a misuse of the time."

Roz is very aware of things like the most efficient use of time, and she keeps strict track of her time every day. When I asked the artists whether they make and stick to schedules, I mentioned an artist I'd interviewed who kept track of every day in fifteen-minute segments. Roz laughed and said, "I don't remember you interviewing me, so I guess it's good to hear that some other

Writing Your Goals

Sit down with your notebook and a pen—and a box of colored pencils or crayons—and make a list of all the goals you'd like to achieve, no matter how far-fetched your logical brain argues they are. Teesha says, "My husband [*artist Tracy V. Moore*] and I have always felt that words were very powerful things. To speak them or write them makes them even more powerful."

If you're like a lot of us, you don't really have any idea what your goals are. You would argue, perfectly convinced, that you don't actually have any. But you do, or you wouldn't be reading this book. Do you want to get back to the painting you put aside after your first job? Do you want to make time to work on your quilt every day? Do you want to set up a studio room where you can leave out all your supplies? Whatever it is that you want to accomplish, that's your first goal.

Try This

Make a list of all the goals you'd like to reach. Never mind how far off or far-fetched they may seem—write them all down and treat each one as if it's a sure thing—remember what Teesha says about the power of words. Pick one that you want to work on right away and then break it down into smaller steps—daily or weekly or monthly or all three. Post the steps on your computer desktop or on your bulletin board. Or both. Write these down in your notebook and carry them with you. For example, let's say you want to make the spare bedroom into a studio. Write that down. Then write the steps you need to take:

- *Clear out boxes in spare bedroom*

- *Go through boxes*

- *Go through closet in spare bedroom*

- *Go through stash of junk under bed in spare bedroom*

- *Sort stuff from spare bedroom: trash, Goodwill, garage sale*

- *Set up garage sale (make this another goal and also start a list for it)*

- *Use profits from garage sale to buy paint for walls of spare bedroom*

- *Figure out storage system for spare bedroom—build or purchase? (Make this into another goal you can break into steps)*

And so on. You get the idea.

Chris Malone

to a different project for the rest of the morning, starting the afternoon perhaps by preparing paper or canvas for several projects because all of that is a similar task and it means one setup time. I like to be really time efficient. It makes me feel happy. I also don't like to be disturbed in my peak hours, so knowing what they are, I don't answer the phone or do e-mails during those times. I save those tasks for when I have low energy or am finished with all my other work. And yes, I like to get to work at the same

How Roz Prepares for a Show

"In 2007 I participated in a group show at the Bell Museum. The group was Project Art for Nature, a group of Minnesota and Wisconsin artists interested in nature and environmental issues. Each of the twenty-five or so artists had a natural area they were studying over time. Since we knew about the show over a year in advance, I knew that I wanted to plan what I showed to reflect my full response to the nature site I'd selected. To this end I knew I wanted to include book projects, paintings and something woven. I planned pieces based on that knowledge and scheduled the making of those items into my work flow. I met that goal with a cohesive group of bird paintings, rock paintings, two book projects—one an artist's book and the other a journal, the two types of book-arts work I'm involved in—and one woven basket. All this happened while I was living my life and doing other work. It was possible for me to do this because I planned and set goals for myself."

artist keeps a time card in fifteen-minute increments! I do that; I have my entire adult life. In part I need to do this because in my design business, time put into a job relates directly to the amount you can bill. I'm also a big fan of scheduling things. After a lifetime of keeping track of how long things take, I can extrapolate pretty accurately on the processes. Because I can extrapolate how long things will take for each part of the process, I can break things down into component bits and schedule them in an efficient manner. And it means that I can work on many projects in a day, doing different parts of one project in a couple hours in the morning, switching time every day. I've always had a schedule. Before I had dogs it was wake up early and go run ten miles, then shower, eat and work. Then when I had dogs it was get up and walk, shower, eat, work, go walking again, work, go walking again, eat, work, go walking again. By the time I got to bed I'd been walking and working the dogs for four hours and been able to get in ten hours minimum of work time at the computer and in the studio." While it may sound exhausting to some of us, Roz's methods of time management allow her to work at all the things she loves.

Making Sure It All Gets Done

When you think of "schedule," it's easy to move right into "goals." All that planning and organizing—it all just fits together. Like everything else, though, there's no consensus. Chris, our Man of Few Words, says he doesn't have any examples of goals because he's right in the middle of getting ready for a show. It's a method that works well for lots of people: Rather than planning and setting goals, they just keep at it, making deadlines and signing contracts and then doing the work.

Judy Wise says, "Well, you might call them 'goals,' but I call them deadlines. I work hard to keep promises and make deadlines. If you don't keep promises to yourself—and others—you soon know that your word is good for nothing. I can't imagine anything worse if you want to be in business. So I guess my rule is that a hard deadline comes before anything."

Lisa says, "Timing long-term goals is difficult for me now. At fifty, I can't live like I'm twenty any more. For example, I have an agreement with the CFM Gallery in New York to do a one-woman show. Neil Zukerman and I have been friends for many years, and we have a good relationship—so much so that I now have an exclusive with him. When we negotiated this show, one provision was that there would be no deadline until a good portion of the work was done. That has been a real lifesaver."

Judy Perez says, "I do not set goals in the traditional

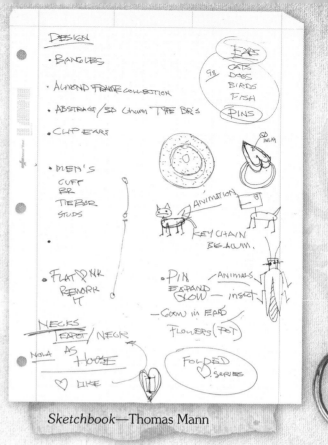

Sketchbook—Thomas Mann

sense. There are things that I would like to do or achieve and I do things that hopefully keep me on track with reaching those things; but I don't aggressively push myself in a conscious way. I sort of feel like if something is meant to be, it will happen when the time is right." This works perfectly for many people, especially those who have a clear idea about where they want to go and the self-discipline to do what needs to be done to get there. Sometimes, though, having a plan really helps to move things a long.

Tom says, "I had a ten-year plan that was completed in 2000. Since then, I've been floundering about, rudderless, just following the course of events—9/11, then Katrina and other personal traumas. Now it's time, in this 'nexus,' to formulate new directions, which seem to be clarifying themselves and revealing the path."

Carter says, "In terms of long-term goals, I'm not exactly sure where I want to go, other than I know that I want to keep making jewelry, and the only way that I can find the time to keep doing this is if I keep selling it. So I need to stay on top of my hill. I need to constantly be trying new things, gaining new ground, and reaching out to the world around me."

Theo also makes the distinction between long- and short-term goals, saying, "I have a long-term goal for the overall direction I'd like to take my work in the coming years. I feel like a lot of the work I've done so far has been preparing me for the longer stories I'd like to tell. My short-term goal is to put more and more of my focus on storytelling. It's easy for it to take a back-seat to art shows and illustrations, because those things are easy in comparison; but storytelling is by far the most important

Flying Lessons—Judy Wise

aspect of my art to me. Over the past couple of years, trying to make a living has been overshadowing my stories. It's been my daily goal to steer my focus back to writing and drawing comics as much as possible."

Being clear about your intentions is a good habit to cultivate. Many people have found it invaluable. Teesha says, "Goals are *so important*. I write things in my

journal and on notepads. I have found that this helps things be realized as well. For instance, I have been 'wishing' for things in my journal—just writing things that come to mind—and I suddenly realized that they all were coming true. Some of these things I wasn't even sure I really wanted, but there I was, in the middle of a trip to Tokyo because I had been 'thinking' about going there on the pages of my journal."

Susan confesses, "I am a calendar junkie! I write lists on paper and stick them on my calendar, keep a notepad on my computer desktop to list goals and deadlines. I have a calendar on my door of my condo where I can see two months at a time and keep on track with deadlines and goals. I have weekly goals that I write down on my calendar—I don't like to have daily goals because I feel like I am pressuring myself. I try and list what I would like to accomplish in a year's time. If they don't get accomplished, they are passed on to the next year. Some of my goals were to run my own online classes off of my Web site, start a newsletter, start teaching out-of-state workshops, having more shows, take a workshop once a year, getting a bigger studio space, and getting my work published. These were goals I had in 2007, and they have been checked off of my list. Most of my goals aren't detail specific, and I work with what I get because I do believe one thing leads to something else that will be even better!"

Traci says, "I try to keep organized by making lists of weekly and monthly to-do's. I also use calendars. I keep different lists for project ideas, blog posts, marketing and business goals. In my purse, I carry a Moleskine mini journal and calendar that is used as a notebook, journal, sketchbook, idea/brainstorm book and expense book. I use Post-It tabs to keep sections separated in the journal. I glue in interesting findings, staple in business cards, brainstorm project ideas, write down phone messages, glue in calendars, put Post-It reminders, collect receipts and tape in inspirational images. Sometime, I collage the covers with my artwork or other papers I've collected during the month. Usually one journal lasts for a month or two. For creative projects, I keep an inspiration board, notebook, or file for each of my projects. I collect color swatches, images, photographs, text, and notes related to the themes of the projects and either paste them onto a board or put them in a notebook."

Pam says, "Sometimes I think what I'm doing is organic planning, because it's not linear, but fluid; and many things have multi-spokes and are intertwined. I have several different ways to plan related to goals—for shows that I want to enter, or shows I've already committed to, I use MacJournal on my laptop to keep track of deadlines, since there are many steps involved in exhibition that each have deadlines—for instance, sign-

Trixie and Rocky—Lisa Lichtenfels

ing contracts, sending digital images, sending artist's bio, résumé and other information, and, of course, shipping the actual work."

So. You've got your list of goals. You know what you want to do, and you've cleared out some time to do it. All you need to do is begin, right? Sometimes that's easy, and sometimes—well, read on.

Chapter 4
Stuck in Time
When You Need a Tow Truck to Get Out of a Rut

You've somehow cleared a luxurious space of several free, uninterrupted hours. You have everything you need. The studio is quiet, and you're ready to begin. You take a deep breath and gaze around you at all your tools and supplies, all carefully arranged, waiting for you.

And nothing happens. No ideas. No spark. No can't-wait-to-get-started galvanic energy. Nothing. If you're like most of us, you might begin to beat yourself up, just the tiniest little bit. You think, "This never happens to anyone else—this doesn't happen to other artists. This never happens to—eeeek!—*Real* Artists!" Ergo, your brain tells you, you must not be a Real Artist. Or maybe you *were*, but now you're not. Maybe (and here's the real fear, the Big Fear) everything has left you and you'll never make art again. You're stuck in time, and you're feeling pretty much all alone, as if your inability to find a focus is your very own dirty little secret.

It's not a secret, and you're not alone. It happens to other artists, too.

True, it doesn't happen to everyone, no. When I asked the artists if they ever find themselves adrift, with plenty of time and everything they need to work but just no impetus to get in there and get started, some of them were truly baffled.

Tom said simply, "I wish!" being unable to conceive of having so much time in the studio that he'd be unable to fill it. Roz and Traci said pretty much the same thing, and Judy Perez added, "Maybe once the kids are grown up and on their own, I may experience that; but so far every free moment is precious." For these artists, that feeling of ennui or boredom is an unknown. We will love them in spite of this, however.

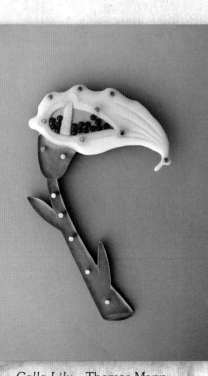

Calla Lily—Thomas Mann

Pesky Men—Pam RuBert

Pam says, "My mom said when I was a kid, I was always busy doing something: making things, doing projects. She said once I told her I was bored, and that's when she knew I was really sick, because, normally, I was always occupied doing, making, reading, drawing, painting something." For her, there's always something she can't wait to do.

The rest of us, though? Sometimes we just feel stuck in time and need a little jump start. Even though Pam never gets stuck, she knows lots of other artists who do; and it's something she's thought quite a bit about.

Pam's Suggestion

"I think you must allow time for creativity before you use up all your juices, and if that means putting off things like laundry or dishes or cleaning or bill-paying, then put it off. You know eventually that sort of stuff is going to get done; so save it for later when your brain is tired from creating, because doing laundry is not brain surgery. You can do that stuff in your sleep. Play before Work—I know this goes against probably everything you've ever been told, but sometimes if I work before play, my play brain is all dried up and just old grumpy work brain is left."

57

BAD IDEA

TAKING HOME THINGS YOU FOUND AT THE BEACH

Bad Idea—Judy Wise

the world that I deserve this creative space and time. And my husband/brother/wife/daughter is going to really love what I've made.' You can't think like that or you will freeze up before you ever put the paintbrush to the canvas. You will be self-editing before you ever start. Or c) sometimes I have a variation on this problem, but it's not necessarily a blank wall or artist's block; but I'm in the middle of a multi-step project—and believe me, there are multi-multi steps in making a big art quilt—and I hit a step that's hard or I'm not clear in my head how to do it, or I get just plain lazy. Somehow that's when either some sort of self-discipline has to kick in—'Sit yourself down, Pam, and finish that drawing'—or I have to realize that maybe this isn't the time or place for it. Maybe I don't have all my ideas clear yet—so what I need to do is some research, like looking on the Internet for examples of exotic bugs to draw, or go to a hair salon and sketch what people really look like when they are having their hair

She says, "I think sometimes that happens because a) they've either worked so hard to clear out all their noncreative obligations, duties and responsibilities first and that has so much tapped them out of energy that when they allow themselves the time and space to create, they are dried up or burnt out. Or b) people hit a blank wall because they have too high of expectations. They work really hard to get this free time set up for creativity, and this great creative space, and then they walk into it saying to themselves, 'OK, today I'm going to paint the Mona Lisa. Or write the great American Novel. Or win a prize. Or get in an important art show. Or create this wonderful thing that is going to prove to

Try This

When you begin a project, what do you need to have? Do you work best from notes? Sketches? A maquette or a muslin (preparatory models)? Do you like to have a checklist of the steps, or do you need to have all your supplies laid out neatly on your work table? Maybe you'd rather just jump in: Just walk into your studio and start pulling fabric off the shelves, taking out paint jars as you need them, all completely spontaneous. In your notebook, make some lists, noting the things you need to have on hand to begin. If your work requires research, make sure to list that.

The Sacred Tree Relocation Project—
Theo Ellsworth

colored, or look at catalogs of furniture for ideas about what would be an interesting chair or lamp to include in a scene. Or maybe my idea's not very good and I should just dump it for something better. Or maybe I don't really have all the materials that I really need yet. Maybe the color scheme in a quilt isn't really working because I don't have the right colors. Or the fabric that I do have is too small to really work for my BIG idea, but I haven't quite realized it yet. So what I really need to do is to find more fabric."

Pam continues, "The other thing I can do is find some other part of the process that happens to be more motivating that day, like dyeing or painting some fabric. There are often steps in the project that can be done

concurrently; or, if not, you can work on several projects at once, and when you get stuck on one, give it a rest and let your subconscious work on it. Pick up another project that seems to be a little easier and make progress on it, go with the path of least resistance. Eventually you'll get several projects done; it just may take a little longer. And sometimes one project will inform another—you may discover a technique in one project that will help another. I've set up my studio so that I can work on several quilts at once, and of course on my computer and sketchbooks. I have many drawings in progress all the time."

Carter Seibels

If this feeling is way too familiar to you, go back and think about what we discussed in Chapter 1, about staying in that right-brain, creative state of mind as much as possible. When you've got ideas perking along all the time—while you're driving the car pool or sitting in a staff meeting or watering the lawn—you're less likely to find yourself faced with a free hour and no ideas to fill it.

The rest of the artists know firsthand about that stuck-in-a-rut feeling, that sense of being blocked. Some have learned to head it off, and some have learned to just go with it, recognizing it as part of an endless cycle.

Judy Wise says, "I think that's normal. I think there is a natural ebb and flow to the creative process. No one gets to be 'on' all the time; that's not how the muse works. In all of nature you see the cycles of abundance and rest. On the days when you feel bored or dead inside, you need to get outside and change things around. Go for coffee, buy art supplies, visit a friend, do some of the routine jobs in the studio that need to be done, like cleaning, organizing, cutting mats, etc. Ride it out."

Theo agrees about that ebb and flow. He says, "As I see it, we as artists have an ongoing working relationship with our own imaginations, and with any long-term—life-long—relationship, there's going to be a waxing and waning. The big thing is to just keep showing up. When you're making a long journey on foot, you're going to hit some rugged terrain, some beautiful vistas and some desolate, muddy vacant lots. All of this becomes valuable when you see it all as part of the creative process. And your work can only become richer for having stuck with it. I feel like our own art is always trying to tell us something, and doing the work is the act of listening." That's a beautiful way to put it, and thinking about it in those terms takes away a lot of the scariness, doesn't it?

Teesha says, "I have had a very few times in my life when I had a lot of time on my hands to make art . . . and I have to say that it feels uncomfortable to me. I like having lots of projects in the air spinning all at once. Doing more energizes me and keeps me from getting bored with doing the same thing. When things have been moving too slowly, I take charge again. I endeavor to make plans to get back into a full menu of activity. My enthusiasm returns, and I become lost in the madness of obses-

Try This

How do you think of these lulls, these slow times? Are they frightening, sending you into a panic? Try looking at them as Theo does—as necessary parts of the journey. The next time you feel you can't get started, think about what part of the journey this might be—the desert, where you might find an oasis? The muddy vacant lot with a leafy park right around the corner? Look at it with a sense of adventure.

sion about things. But I love it. I thrive on it." For Teesha, having so many things to do that there's not enough time to do them is key; rather than clearing out her schedule, she adds to it to get that sense of being overwhelmed that she finds essential to creativity.

For Carter, a bit of dead time is actually a harbinger of good times. She says, "This seems to happen when I have not been giving myself enough creative play time—when I let other things take over. So the ideas have not been flowing. And then I get a chunk of time to explore, and the ideas are all dried up! It's awful. But a good creative challenge. I find that oftentimes my best ideas come after these dry spells. I have this theory that it takes ideas a while to come to the surface. It had to happen to me lots of times before I noticed the trend, but I find that when I have a creative 'dry spell,' I get in a funk, am in a bad mood, things aren't going my way. I'm just not having a good time with my work. And then all of a sudden, it's like a volcano erupting—the ideas start flowing. It's like the magma coming to the surface—the ideas have to work their way from the subconscious to the conscious before they can reveal themselves to you! No matter how painful the dry spell has been, the creativity always returns; and I am always left feeling more satisfied than before after the birth of another new idea."

Sometimes the same thing can happen at the end of a period of ideas and hard work, when you're just worn out and need to let that right brain rest a little. Lori says, "Occasionally, I get a little blocked and feel overwhelmed with an oversupply of time and, less often, materials. This tends to happen at the end of a long creative spurt, and my mind or spirit needs a little break. I think these 'blocks' are part of the creative cycle and I welcome them. Sometimes I need to exercise a different part of my brain that doesn't benefit from making things—the part that thrives on organization and process. When I feel blocked or uninspired, I tend to do process-oriented things like organizing, sorting, cleaning, ironing—things that I am able to control and manipulate. For some reason, this relaxes the other side of my brain that just wants to get lost in that 'zone.'" Handling the materials is a huge help for lots of artists—just getting in there and re-folding the fabric, working the clay, sharpening the pencils. And cleaning, even though that's seldom anyone's first choice, as Susan explains.

"When I really get in a slump, I will go for a walk. I take my camera along and just start snapping photos of interesting 'stuff.' I will cull through

Lolita—Lori Sandstedt

Lisa's Story

"When I found my direction, it became a focus for my entire life. I had been working at the Disney Studios as an animator. Unfortunately, I was working my way up as an 'inbetweener.'" "In-betweeners" do the countless drawings between the key drawings of their superior boss animator. Say, he would do drawings #1, 15, 32, 57, and 104. You had to fill in all the rest. It used your capacity as an artist but gave no freedom for creation. I did this for months until one day I couldn't get the pencil to touch the paper. It was like I was trying to push two magnets together. As hard as I tried, I couldn't get that pencil to touch the paper. It was then that I realized I was having a nervous breakdown. How was I going to exist at Disney if I couldn't get paper and pencil to get along?

"It was the end of my dream, and also my father's. He had helped design the monorail for the original Disneyland in California, and I remember meeting Walt Disney as a very small child. My father was never so proud as when I got a great job at Disney—all the money he thought he threw away on art college was miraculously vindicated. He never forgave me for leaving Disney; and he died shortly after that, very disappointed with his wayward daughter.

"The next thing I know, Jerry and I were in an old Ford van with everything we owned crammed in and on top of it, with my Chevette Scooter equally packed towed behind us. As we left Los Angeles and started climbing over the Rocky Mountains, I experienced a kind of lightness of being. It would take many years of working out, but I was on my way to living as an artist."

Josephine—Lisa Lichtenfels

all of my art magazines, Web sites, and books to see if anything jumps out at me. I keep an art journal and will cut and paste photos of objects or artworks that catch my eye. Doodling in my art journal is a good jump-starter. There are times I will order new materials and books to teach myself a new technique. If all else fails, I start cleaning! I will get in my studio and start pulling stuff out of the shelves. I will find materials I have stored away and forgotten about. Getting my studio space in order is always good for my creative spirit."

For Kelly, it's often just playing with the materials in a completely nonpressured way. She explains what it's like when she can't get things going: "This happens to me for a variety of reasons. One: I haven't created anything in a long time, and I feel unsure of what to begin. Two:

I'm intimidated by a blank white canvas and have no idea what to do, usually based in fear of doing something wrong or messing it up. Three: I'm experiencing burnout and my inspiration is blah. I also think that a blank white canvas, if you're painting, can be quite paralyzing. Where to start? What should I do? Sometimes I think we get so intimidated by the creative process that we get fearful about simply beginning. When I turn on the music and

Traci's Graffiti Canvas

Here's an exercise from Traci that not only gets you moving but can sometimes provide the beginnings of a project itself.

Put a large sheet of brown craft paper or watercolor paper up on the wall. Put a cup of pens, markers, pencils or tools next to it and do these exercises:

• Write the alphabet large without lifting your pen

• Make a list of creative words, to-do's, places where you want to travel

• Write the definitions of words on your paper

• Scrape paint on the background

• Scribble with a black marker all over the paper, and layer with more pen or pencil scribbles in different colors

• Dip a brush or skewer in ink and make marks on the paper

• Take a photo of your wall art and alter it in Photoshop

• Cut up the paper for pieces of collage

Brave—Kelly Rae Roberts

Chris Malone

just take the approach of 'I'm playing today. This is all about having fun, experimenting, making mistakes,' then I'm able to move past it and start creating. All in all, I think it's important that we simply show up at the table and simply begin—even on the days we don't really want to. For me, it's much like going to the gym. It's sometimes really hard for me to get there, but once I'm there, I feel so much better than I did. One thing that has worked for me is focusing on creating backgrounds. Instead of worrying about what my painting will look like in the end, I just play with paint and paper and start creating messy, free-spirited and colorful backgrounds. Sometimes, when I'm really stuck, I'll spend the entire day making backgrounds, loving every minute of it because the internal pressure is released. I'm having fun, and the ideas start flowing again—often the minute I put color onto a white canvas."

Pam finds inspiration in her materials, too—and that doesn't include just the fabric she uses on her quilts.

"Materials are very important to an artist. That's also one of the problems of being an artist—you tend to want to save everything because 'you might one day use it for some art.' At least it is with me—I have tons of crazy stuff, boxes of little vintage soaps that someone collected from hotels all over the country. What am I ever going to do with that? Stacks of old magazines from the '50s. We have probably a thousand spindles of different shapes and sizes that came off of old stair rails, boxes of magnetic letters that I like to spray paint and stick to metal file cabinets, old typewriters. Well, you get the idea—that's some of what's filling up a 22,000 square foot factory and warehouse. I also have a term for organizing materials—I call

Cicada House—Judy Coates Perez

it 'borging,' after the Star Trek species who kidnap and convert people and other species and adapt them to fit into their 'collective' beehive that floats around space in a big metal cube. Kind of gory, I know; but whenever I buy fabric or collect other materials, I have to wash and iron it, or if it's boxes of old ephemera, sort through what I think is relevant and toss the rest. And if I've finished a big project, there's usually a lot of stuff strewn around, so I have to organize it and borg it back into the collective. You know, make it mind! Anyway, sorting and organizing materials is a way to re-acquaint yourself with interesting things you had forgotten you had because it somehow got jammed under the sofa when you were cleaning up in a hurry. It can also inspire new ideas, or maybe help you to see how you've moved on and don't really need some of it anymore and can toss it. It can help you see what is missing from your collection and motivate you to go out and get it—maybe you haven't been painting because you need more red acrylic, or your brushes are getting ratty."

While cleaning and organizing your studio is often just what you need—because there's nothing like dusting to make your mind come up with alternatives in a hurry—sometimes staying in the studio is the worst thing you can do. Like Judy Wise said, sometimes you need to get outside. Theo says, "I like going on long walks. I like to just leave my house and start walking, without paying too much mind to where I'm going. It's a good way to relax my thoughts and let my mind wander and my eyes observe. I like going to a hilly city park near my house. I usually bring a notebook and pen, just in case. I like riding my bike and getting some kind of exercise." Getting away for an hour or an afternoon can be just what you need. When Chris needs to get away, he's got a city full of places to go.

"When I was just getting started, I would go to museums—Washington, D.C., has a wealth of museums. I would also people watch, as museums such as the Smithsonian and the National Gallery draw people from all over the world. A lot of times, I would just sit quietly and block out all of the nonsense around me. I would let inspiration come."

Judy Perez recommends museums, too. She says, "Get out and see art, not just the media that you prefer to work in. Go to art museums and galleries. Make a notebook with images and colors that appeal to you, and don't be conscious of the source. I find that everything I do influences something else. When I feel stuck creatively, I knit, look through my sketchbooks, look at art and nature books or films with lots of visuals. I also switch mediums and work in something unrelated to my usual work. I try and push myself out of my comfort zone."

Sometimes the problem isn't that you don't have a project you want to work on but that it's just hard to get started every day. Pam knows that feeling, and she says, "One of the best ideas for keeping the flow going during a big project I got from Twyla Tharp's book *The Creative Habit*. She calls it building a bridge, and suggests finding a stopping place at the end of each work session, when you're not completely tired and you have in mind the next step that you are going to make. That way you leave the studio with optimism and looking forward to work the next day. Then the next time you walk into the stu-

dio, you can jump right into that next step without losing the flow of work on your projects. This has worked very well for me, especially keeping me on a roll during a long project." It worked well for Ernest Hemingway, too—he always stopped writing for the day when he knew exactly what was going to happen next. Knowing what comes next is often all it takes to keep the necessary focus, which, of course, is critical.

Lisa says, "If an artist finds he or she can't work or focus, they are in trouble—kinda like a professional athlete who breaks a leg. Just because it is psychological doesn't make it less real. Years ago, before I started doing the work that is my calling, I would have agonizing times when I couldn't get it going. Much of my college years were spent in this agony, and I have great compassion for any creative person in this situation. On the one hand, I was trying everything, and it was exciting, especially learning new mediums and experiencing new directions. But doing art and learning are two very different things. Occasionally I will get off track. This only happens when some psychological violence has been done to me. When Jerry had a heart attack in 1994, I was horrified—not only with his illness and brush with death, but that I could no longer work or think as an artist. I was almost without him, and without myself."

Does that help? Maybe this was all you needed to get going—just knowing that you're not alone and that, whatever hour of the day or night you're sitting down to begin a project, there are others out there doing the same thing, struggling with the same hurdles, wrestling with the same issues. You're not alone, and it's all going to be OK.

Princess Arsinoe in the Ostrich Race—Lisa Lichtenfels

Chapter 5

Jumpstarting Time

A Nudge to Get Going When You're Spinning Your Wheels

 Sometimes it's not that you can't get started at all. Starting is not the problem. Rather, you find yourself spinning your wheels, doing the same thing over and over and over, going to your studio and falling into the same old creative rut. It sounds like an oxymoron, doesn't it? "Creative rut." But what it means is that your creativity is still there; it's just not going anywhere. The resulting feelings are much the same as those that plague you when you can't get started: You start to question your creativity, wondering if you'll ever have a great idea ever again. You fear that you're just one step away from turning into one of those people you've seen at art fairs who show up year in and year out with a booth full of work that looks exactly like what they were making a dozen years ago. It's terrifying to contemplate, isn't it? Don't despair. Cre-

Mysterious Migration—Pam RuBert

ative ruts lie in wait for everyone, no matter how terrific their work or prodigious their creativity or stellar their track record of having new ideas.

Chris says, "I stay true to my creativity, and I think one's work will mature if you are honest with yourself. I don't stir things up intentionally, but my work does demand a reaction; and you want your work to 'grab' people." When you have a following, a group of people who collect your work and are always waiting to see what you're going to do next, there's the additional pressure of trying to stay one step ahead of yourself. Listen to the firsthand accounts of two artists who have just pulled themselves out of pretty deep ruts.

Roz: Steering Around Ruts

"I don't think of myself as getting into creative ruts, but I do love to set myself up with projects that I know would help folks in a creative rut, so perhaps I just am always making preemptive strikes! I think some people try to shake things up and get out of ruts without really delving deeply enough into something. I think that daily practice of at least a month on a project is needed.

"I did a thirty-birds-in-thirty-days painting project last year. I limited it in the following ways:

• Had to use only supplies on hand (I had a bunch of small canvases left over from another project)

• Had to be small

• Had to be acrylic paint (paint I already had—no buying more, except I did buy some more Titanium White)

• Had to use drawings I'd already done in my journals (this was essential to limit the time spent each day)

• Had to work on a color theory issue

• Had to resist the urge to work tightly! I wanted those paintings to be looser than my usual work.

"The result was thirty paintings that I really enjoy for different reasons. And some new understanding about paint colors that I normally wouldn't have used."

She pauses, thoughtful, and then adds, "I think yes, I do intentionally shake things up. I do this by keeping a journal. It's the most subversive art tool I know of. I think my journal is a built-in rut buster. I'm always trying out new things in my journal, always experimenting, always documenting how a painting is going so I can get the same effect if I want to use it again or so I can teach something so that it is repeatable for the students. Because of this I really do believe my journal is constantly taking me new and exciting places."

69

Kelly says, "I get tired, restless, bored with what I've been painting; and the friction starts to pull at me. This also happens when I've been spending too much time on my creative business and not enough time doing the other things I enjoy that make me, *me*—writing, exercising, time with family and friends, reading, etc. When this happens, I need to take a break and acknowledge that yes, this feeling is called burnout; and it's OK to give myself permission to rest. It's in times of rest that my creativity gets to breathe a bit deeper, and I begin to see and notice things I wasn't able to before when I was in a dark rut. I'm actually just coming out of a pretty exhausting burnout, and I'm noticing now how much better I feel with a couple weeks of resting—no painting, minimal creative business work and a media cleanse—no e-mail or blog reading. Already, my inspiration is returning and the ideas are flowing again."

Carter says, "I spent the last year or so in a creative rut. I had one of those years where my jewelry wasn't selling very well, so I didn't make any new beads or new styles. And because I wasn't making new jewelry, I wasn't selling anything. And because I was a bit put out by the whole scenario, I was turning to other things to create: PMC (precious metal clay), resin, metalsmithing, altered artwear . . . I was looking all around me for

Carter Seibels

other things to try besides bead making because it had become stagnant for me. I wasn't allowing myself much time at the torch to play, so the beads were boring. It was one of those vicious cycles, but for some reason it took me quite some time to realize this. I think I was letting myself get too focused on the selling of my work rather than the creating of my work; and instead of challenging myself creatively in my art form—lampworking—I was bouncing around to other things to satisfy my need for a creative outlet." The whole making-art-and-making-a-living combination can cause all kinds of rut-inducing problems. If you're selling your work, you're reluctant to change things too much: your customers might hate the new direction. Yet, on the other hand, if you don't change, your customers may begin to find your work stale—they've already collected some of it and see no point in buying more that's just the same. You love what you do, but you also have to look at it as a business. Reconciling those two parts of your art can be tough—one of the reasons it's a good idea to stop and think about whether you really want to make art your career or whether you're perfectly content to keep the two completely separate.

Carter adds, "When I stop worrying about it and stop trying to focus too much on having a certain outcome, it comes naturally to me. And then the creativity flows. When I stop trying to make what I think people want to see, when I stop focusing on all of the end details, the new ideas come flowing, and I end up selling the work as well."

Judy Wise says, "I think repeating any great idea for commerce can dig an ugly hole that eventually hurts your soul. No matter how much you need the money, this is not the way to nirvana. Change it up. I've moved from one medium to another several times over the years. That's why I've worked in so many different mediums and why I chose teaching over art fairs recently: a new game, new things to learn, new challenges, friends, locations. I've learned to love risk and all the creative energy that comes with it."

Lisa agrees about the lure of proven financial success, saying, "Creative ruts happen when you do the same thing over and over. You can make a lot of money doing this, and most artists need to do it to some extent in order to survive. Doing something new takes more time and energy than doing what you know. Sadly, doing what you know is very dangerous. The brain can be very lazy—you have to push it to see things as they really are

Heart Pendant—Thomas Mann

Try This

Where do you go for inspiration? Do you, like Tom, have notebooks full of old sketches, drawings and notes? Do you have art books that never fail to spark new ideas? Whatever the source, gather these together in one place that's easily accessible. When the rut threatens to swallow you up, spend an evening reacquainting yourself with the ideas on those pages.

instead of what your conscious brain thinks it sees. For me, life is too short to repeat."

Tom also knows all about the demands of doing work for which you've become well known. He says, "The creative rut is always looming. For me, it's called 'Techno-Romantic.' It's always waiting for me to give it some attention, but it's always ready to suck me in and consume all of my creative attention. When I teach my

Discovering Joy—Kelly Rae Roberts

digms on a regular basis, the fact remains that Techno-Romanticism is the identifying feature of my career.

"When the rut looms, I go to the Library. Not the public one, but the personal studio and home one. I have an extensive library of art and art-related books, but the most important documents are those in my own drawing binders. There are so many ideas in those old drawings that I never turned into objects. I never fail to find something that immediately puts me back on the track to a parallel idea or a completely new one."

Sometimes the pressure of having customers waiting to see what's new can be a really good thing, forcing you to rise to the challenge of creating new work, which is often all it takes to keep you going forward. Susan believes it's vital to keep people coming back to see what you're up to. She says, "I know some artists will say, 'I do the art for me and don't care if it sells'—which is great if you aren't worried about paying bills. Art is a business, and you need to know how to keep your customers coming to you and buying more of your work. Also, I like to challenge myself and not get comfortable in my work."

Carter agrees: "Many of my customers are repeat customers, so they like to see new things. Of course they aren't going to buy the same necklace over and over again. So it's important to have an evolution in design." Carter mentioned earlier that she stays on top of the

Design for Survival classes, I suggest to my students that, if you are only able to discover one thing, one technical trick, one design system, one look in your entire artistic career, that is capable of generating income on a regular basis, you should count yourself fortunate. If you come up with more than one, several . . . well, you might be a genius. Well, Techno-Romantic is that for me. And while I exercise vociferously developing other design para-

trends in beads, checking out artists' Web sites and the auctions on eBay, and Susan says, "I watch the trends in art and watch what others are doing."

For other artists, the pressure of the marketplace isn't as intense, for a variety of reasons. Still, while they don't deliberately shake up their work, and while they try not to let outside influences—the market, the audience, possible galleries—force them to make deliberate changes, change does happen, occurring naturally as they work.

Theo says, "As long as I'm engaged by a picture or a story, it feels fresh to me. I try not to think too much about what other people will think of it. The work evolves as I go and unexpectedly leads to new places. I just try to listen and respond to new ideas as they come. When I'm working on a comic story, I end up adding spontaneous ideas that come to me while I'm drawing. I like to keep the process as spontaneous as possible."

That sense of being in the process, of following the work as it evolves, is one Kelly relishes. She says, "For me, I keep it fresh by enjoying the process. The minute I'm not enjoying myself, my work feels spiritless, and I

Try This

What scares you, artistically? In your notebook, make a list of the things that both attract you and scare you, whatever they are. They could be techniques, such as soldering or encaustic; or they could be challenges such as entering a juried show or building a Web site. Make several lists if you need to. Then pick one thing to tackle. Don't pick the one that seems easiest; pick the one that seems scary but also a whole lot of fun.

Lisa's Story

Lisa tells of the advice she got years ago from Eric Larson, one of the "Nine Old Men" at Disney. Tasked with making a short film to show her stuff, Lisa found herself asking how to make something new, how to shake things up and impress the big boys.

Eric said, "Do you know what makes a great animator? A great artist knows how to throw everything away. You throw away the world around you, and you even throw away who you are. The only thing that matters is the character. You have to become the character. You can't animate without being the character. If you are the character, everything falls into place."

Lisa says, "The first time I accomplished working the way Eric told me to work, I was doing a portrait of Eleanor Roosevelt. I showed the piece at an exhibition in New England and was approached by a woman who had been working on a painting of Eleanor for several years. She asked me about nuances I had captured in my fabric sculpture that amazed her because she had never noticed those things before, even though she had studied the face for such a long time. Actually, I didn't realize I had put them there until she pointed them out. I'm not sure about this, but I think that when you become the character, as Eric described, you tap into your unconscious or subconscious mind. It is a wonderful way to work; but, of course, there are, as with everything, downsides. While I was Eleanor, I joined several political groups and civic organizations. When I was no longer Eleanor, well, Jerry was very good to go and make my apologies and erase my name from the lists. When you slip in and out of persona, it's nice to have a caretaker. Jerry is a very good one."

Strength—Judy Wise

to live with the work—and the process of creating the work—day in and day out. If it's not fresh and exciting for them, it's just not going to keep happening. If you're engaged and excited and enthusiastic, that will fill up the work you produce.

Pam says, "I think my work continually changes because of the varied lifestyle I live. With travel and constantly exposing myself to new art and artists, I don't see how I could not change; and since I am always changing,

Try This

How can you challenge your "lazy brain" within your medium? If you paint, what thing could you learn that would be just difficult enough you'd have to work at it? If you quilt, what challenge could you set for yourself? Start with thinking about color.

Judy Perez recommends: "People often get in a color rut, always relying on that same tried and true palette they feel comfortable with. The first thing to do is pick the color you like the least and force yourself to work with it in a small format. Do several studies of a particular image or series of images, working with that color, picking colors close to it on the color wheel, then work with the color and its complement/opposite. Often if you work within a very structured set of rules, ideas start popping up of new ways to expand on these ideas. It is almost like working within the box suddenly frees you to work outside the box."

believe it shows in the actual painting. On the flip side, if I'm loving the process of painting, then it shows—that energy and spirit is reflected in the piece." That's a sentiment you hear again and again: The work reflects how you feel about it and about the process of creating it.

Teesha says, "Work stays fresh when you are there for it—when you are fully engaged in what it is that you are doing. I love creating ideas and then making them come into fruition." Her enthusiasm shows in the pieces she creates; for many artists, it's not about making things new and fresh for viewers and buyers; it's about making things fresh for themselves. They're the ones who have

my work will, too. I thrive on incongruity. I think part of creativity is the ability to step out of one's self and look and experience the world from a totally different or unexpected viewpoint. Just like the body isn't healthy when it has the same food day after day, so it is with the spirit and mind."

Some people find that deliberately shaking things up is a really good thing. Judy Perez says, "I consciously think about not wanting to make a piece of art like something that has been seen before. I want to make the unexpected. For example, if there is a request for art with a floral theme, I am not going to make roses and tulips. I am going to take a carnivorous pitcher plant and try to make it a stunning contender for floral beauty." It's not just about changing what you're doing; it's also about changing how you look at what you're doing—and, in the process, changing how others see what you're doing, as well.

Judy Wise says, "Sometimes I just put my foot down with myself: 'No more of such and such.' We all get tired of seeing the same predictable work

from an artist. I have to keep moving, searching, trying new things. I have a very low threshold for boredom. I know that the cycle will pass if I just entertain myself and do something enjoyable instead of trying to be an art drudge. If it isn't fun, it isn't art. Do something else. The muse will be back shortly."

Susan offers advice that has worked for her: "I make it a point to mix it up! I use Picasso as my inspiration, because he would not stay with one style and would try different art mediums. You need

Dita—Lori Sandstedt

to keep variety in your work. Try new materials, read books about new techniques, take a class, do something besides sit there and stare at the piece hoping something will magically appear. Also, I get bored easily, so I make an effort to have several projects going on at one time."

The suggestion to "take a class" may seem simplistic, something that people suggest but that Real Artists never actually do. Listen to Lisa's story. She fell into a rut induced by two different agents vying for her work.

"What I did to get out of it was to stop making art. I took courses in the history and meaning of music. It went all the way back in time to what they know about ancient Greek music, through the Middle Ages—some great polyphony there—and I got to learn what all the 'classical' music was about. By the time we all got the Beethoven, I was ready to go back to work. I don't know why it worked, but it did." Sometimes it's just the change that gets things going, as Teesha explains: "I have learned through the years that I need change. But it doesn't have to be drastic changes; just little things keep me energized and excited. I just change gears. If it is journaling that seems to have

Chris Malone

lost it for me, I start working with fabrics or assemblage work or my current obsession, mobiles, or what I call hanging art. I am constantly doing things a little differently from year to year with my retreats, teaching and my magazine to keep it fresh for me."

Lori says, "I make a variety of things—clothing, handbags, jewelry—and occasionally I feel the need to move from one category into another." For Judy Perez, there's always knitting waiting nearby.

Carter says, "It's where dabbling in other art forms and allowing creative playtime come in, because they are key to keeping the ideas flowing and to not getting bored." Working in different media can do it, and so can working in a series in one medium.

Traci says, "When I am creating art, one strategy for me to keep my work fresh is to work on multiple projects or pieces at once. When I paint and do my collage work, I usually work on five to seven different pieces at once, adding a layer to each as I go."

Traci Bautista

There are all kinds of tricks to avoiding the ruts, and much of the time these are effective. But not always. Sometimes you have to learn ways to haul yourself out after you fall in.

Chris remembers a time, back in his early days of creating figures, when he almost got completely sidetracked into a truly scary rut. "In the beginning when I was making dolls in the '90s when everyone was making fairies and hobgoblins, I jumped on board with that; and it blocked out my own creativity by me not following my own inner creative voice." Fortunately, he escaped and found his own path, about which we all are so very delighted: Many people were making fairies, but no one else creates figures like his. Finding his way out took him in a direction all his own, which seems so simple looking back. Looking back on being in a rut is always so much simpler, though, than looking up when you're firmly stuck deep inside one.

Carter recommends experimenting with color, too: "I like to give myself color combinations to work with. Unexpected colors that I wouldn't normally work with, maybe just four glass rods that are sitting next to each other. I'll make a necklace or a set of beads using those colors. It can be really refreshing for the eye to see different color combinations, and a lot of times I find that's all I need to feel refreshed and get out of my rut."

She adds, "Experimenting is important for any artist. If you just make the same thing over and over again, it becomes rote behavior. Creative exploration is invigorating, exciting and gets good energy flowing so that even when you do have to return to filling orders and building inventory, the enthusiasm is still there and the mind is working on new ideas while the hands go through the motions. I think what I do to get out of the creative rut is quite simply to work through it. You know the saying 'The journey is the reward'—to me that's what being in a creative rut is like: You have to move through it, experience it, learn from it; and then you will come through on the other side with more knowledge about how to move through more quickly and effectively the next time it comes around."

Judy Wise says, "I had normally worked in acrylic but have moved over to the medium of wax—encaustic. I assigned myself some intense learning exercises—had my partner cut up an entire sheet of plywood into 8" × 10" pieces for me to practice on and completed four of these a day for a month until a clear direction emerged. I learned a tremendous amount in that month. In the beginning I looked at that box of plywood pieces and wondered if the end would ever come, but it came; and when all the wood was used up, I was still energized and inspired to do more. It was a month of creative fervor."

Theo says, "Sometimes I'll find myself falling back on some familiar imagery in my drawings, especially if I have to come up with something for an art show on a tight deadline. Deadlines can be creative rut-inducing. I like to put a lot of detail into every piece I do. In my art,

the feeling I crave the most is the feeling of adventure and exploration, so when I find myself falling back on the familiar, I immediately start feeling restless. When this happens, I try to put things into perspective. When outside pressure and deadlines start affecting my work in a negative way, I try to remember why I do what I do. My work has to have that sense of personal investment for me to feel fulfillment. The integrity of the work is more important than any imposed deadline. I try to let go of the pressure and simply start having fun with my work again. I always revert back to my doodling origins and simply start making marks on a piece of paper. Doodling helps me think, gets me back in the zone. I also crave that feeling of breaking new ground. I'm always trying to explore a bit further and discover new things. I get bored when I find myself sticking to the safe, familiar territory. Luckily, there's always something strange and uncharted right around the corner. I just have to keep being open to the process and let my art show the way. Letting myself be playful always leads out of the rut and back to the sense of adventure."

That sense of fun and adventure—that's what it's all about, from the very first mark you ever put on a piece of paper. In learning how to jump-start stalled time, you pick up techniques that allow you to climb up out of the rut and get back to the joy of creating. The best advice, simply put? When you're stuck, go play. Play with your paints, your clay, your fabric—whatever material does it for you. Forget the rules, the lessons, the guidelines you've learned about how to do things and spend a little time in the world of "What if?"

What if I sculpted wood instead of clay?
What if I made a quilt that was octagonal?
What if I painted with only two colors?
What if I . . . ?

Go. Play.

Following the Moon—Judy Wise

Creative Space

And then there's Space. Time and Space—you can't have one without the other, right? Kind of like cosmic peanut butter and jelly. In this second section, we're going to talk about space, and, just as we did with time, we're going to talk about difference kinds. First, in Chapter 6, we're going to talk about mental space, about the space your art and creativity occupy inside your head—and in the priorities you set for your daily life. Do you give them a lot of time, or do they get what's left over after you obsess about your day job and possible periodontal disease? You'll see that our artists give pretty much all of their brain over to their art, but somehow manage to go through most of their days without absentminded mishaps. How does it work? You'll be amazed at what you can do when you start to grant your creativity the space—and the respect—it deserves.

Chapter 7 is all about fun: two really great ways to preserve that precious space in your brain, once you've begun to clear it out and make more room for creative ideas. It's all about play, which is kind of like decorating the space in your head, and journals, which is kind of like the record book for that space, like the visitors' log in a gallery. You have the ideas sign in so you can keep track of them. Then, in Chapter 8, we move back out into the real world and visit actual physical spaces where real artists do their work. They have tips and ideas for you, too, no matter whether your studio is a state-of-the-art custom-designed behemoth or a corner of the kitchen table or a cozy chair pulled up by the window.

And what do you do when you're in that space, ready to get on with it but maybe just having the tiniest bit of trouble signaling your brain that it's time to get to work? In Chapter 9, we talk about studio rituals—all the little habits and quirks that help you fill your space with energy, from lighting a candle to brewing a cup of tea—and do we have tea suggestions for you! Music, too.

Then, in Chapter 10, we talk about the ultimate space: out on the road, out in the world. Not all artists take their works-in-progress out of the studio, but some do; and in this chapter we'll talk vacations and travel journals and working on your art at the local coffee shop—all the things that give you a chance to take your art out in the wider world.

You've made some time; now let's focus our attention on making some space.

Chapter 6

Mental Space

What Goes on Up There in Your Head?

When we talk about having space to make art, we have to talk about two kinds of space. We have to consider the physical space, sure—the desk or table or closet or studio or wherever it is you go when you make things. A lot of people bemoan the lack of space for making art, believing that, if only they had a well-appointed studio somewhere off in the woods, they'd get ever-so-much more stuff done. And it's true that you need some space in which to work. But what's even more true—and what we have to think about before we can think about a room of your own—is that there has to be some mental space given over to your work. Think back to Chapter 1, when we talked about integrating creativity with everything else in your life. It's like that: You need to give your creative life and ideas and odd and fanciful notions enough space in your head so that they're not crowded, so that they have room to expand and fill out and take on shape and form.

James Thurber, the early twentieth-century essayist and humorist, said that he was always writing, no matter what he appeared to be doing. He might seem to be chatting at a cocktail party or sitting at the table having dinner; but, in his head, he was writing. It's like that for a lot of creative people: No matter what mundane tasks are requiring their physical presence, their brains are involved in writing or painting or stitching or drawing or just coming up with fanciful ideas that have nothing to do with the task at hand. It's what makes many artists seem a little absent-minded because, well, they are. They've wandered off in their heads to a part of their brain that's filled with quirky ideas and things they want to try. Forget the guest speaker at the annual retreat; you're thinking about Japanese wax-resist.

Because the artists here are working artists and making their art is their career, their work takes up a considerable amount of the space in their head. Yours may not require quite as much, but the more room in your brain you can give over to creative ideas, the more those ideas will be able to flourish. They need room to breathe!

One of the biggest problems with granting creativity enough space in your thoughts and in your life is that it's not seen as being valuable. Creativity is often an afterthought, something you think about in your spare time, something you'll devote more thought to later, on the weekend or on vacation or when the kids are grown or when you retire.

This is nonsense. Creativity is stunningly important, as important as almost anything else you can name except maybe food, water, and shelter. Think about how you feel when things are so hectic and crazy that you don't have time to even think about making anything, much less actually getting into the studio. Your brain

of those daydreams and flights of imagination as being unimportant or expendable. Instead, recognize them for what they are: an absolutely indispensable part of you and your creative life.

Susan says, "My mind is always working! I see ideas on TV and in movies, advertising, magazines and life. I am always looking for my next project. When I wake up in the morning and go to bed at night, I lie in the bed and get my mind around what I am working on or problem solve. It is like a meditation of sorts."

Because clothing and fashion and style are omni-present, Lori finds herself constantly immersed in what she loves. "I think a lot about fashion and design. I pay

Funky Fungus—Susan Sorrell

is completely occupied with work and family and the chores of daily living. How do you feel? If you're like most of us, you feel just the tiniest bit nuts. Kind of off-kilter, and maybe as if your soul has been ripped out of your body. In a very real way, it has: Your creativity is a vital part of you, one you need to be a fully functioning human being. Without it, you're that proverbial shell of a person. You need it, and it needs you: Your creative ideas need to be given the space, time and respect something so important deserves to have in your life. So don't think

That Space in Your Brain

In that little notebook you've gotten used to slip-ping in your pocket, make a time grid for the day, marking off each hour and leaving enough space to jot down words to keep track of what goes on in your head. What do you think about all day long? What's up there when you're driving? When you're washing dishes? Feeding the dog? Are you fully present in each moment, thinking about the turn signals and the grease-cutting suds and whether Spot is getting a little paunchy? If so, good for you. But if you find yourself thinking about other random things—weather-stripping, or picking up the dry cleaning—you've got some mental space that's waiting to be filled with something wonderful. For now, just note what's up there, jotting down a word or two to remind you later.

attention to what people wear. How do they choose? Comfort? Color? Utility? I realize a lot of people care little about what they wear, but I'm still fascinated by their choices. Frequently, when I should be listening to the dialogue of a movie, I'm taking in the background scenery, thinking about set design, why they chose that particular drapery for the windows. My husband Carl probably gets tired of my commentary about which colors don't

Graven Images—Judy Coates Perez

Roz and Imperfection

"Having the car accident was also a big learning piece for me. It was something I couldn't control, and I couldn't control the aftermath and toll it took on my body. A very wise person noticed how rigid I was getting after the accident. She told me to think about this, 'What could I get accomplished today if I let go of perfect?' She isn't the first person to say this, or the last, but she said it to me at a point in my life when I could hear it. After a lifetime of being perfectly capable in all aspects of my life, things had ground to a halt. For someone who has defined herself by her productivity from the age of five, this physical reality was crushing. This friend's comment helped me find my way back from that."

flatter the news anchor's skin tone. I can't help myself. Those things are just always on my mind."

Judy Perez says, "Oh, that Thurber example feels exactly like me! I think it is hard for me to separate myself from the creative. As I go through life, I often derive imagery and ideas from everyday life. Sometimes from books that I am reading or my personal interests; but most often, I am inspired by my kids. When we lived in Austin, Texas, my son was really into fossils. After spending many afternoons walking down Shoal Creek looking for fossils,

I was inspired to make *Primordial Sea*. This quilt is my vision of what the ocean once covering Texas may have looked like. I thought about how to make this quilt a long time, collecting images and writing down ideas, finally deciding on dyeing silk charmeuse to shimmer like water with imagery painted with textile paints and plankton quilted into the water. My son also loved lichen—he collected these lovely little lacey forms and laid them on the front porch. The colors

Portrait of a Garden Gnome—
Theo Ellsworth

Theo and Inner Space

"I try to relate to people and the world from the same place that I related to my art from. I do my best not to be distant and off in my own head when I'm around other people. I like to be present and engage when I'm in social situations. I love talking to people! But I also need and crave alone time to the point of being protective of it. I like having periods of time where I'm simply unable to be contacted. Without that time to myself, experiencing my own creative inner space, it's hard for me to feel social. On my ideal days, I'm able to create a balance between my need to work alone and my desire to nurture a sense of community in my life. I don't like to see everything else as secondary to my art, but my art *is* me, and it's at the center and the soul of everything I do. So unless I'm living up to my art, and being true to what my work wants to express through me, I end up feeling incredibly awkward and out of place in the world. I need to be making art to feel at home here."

Traci Bautista

idea comes and I mull it over in my mind, before I have figured out what it should be and start putting pencil to paper, and the hours spent lying in bed at night working out the process in my mind? For me, the idea, image or story I am trying to convey is a huge part of the overall art, so I spend a lot of time thinking about the idea. Is it worthwhile, or visually compelling? Often when I have an idea for a new quilt I think about it for up to a year before I start. I begin collecting 'scrap'—pictures of animals, plants or figures—to reference when beginning the design, and images that maybe inspire the style and color or atmosphere of the piece."

Pam says, "I'd say that pretty much I live and breathe art, and to me art is a subset of creativity. Pretty much I think about it all the time and always am trying to inter-ject creativity into whatever I do. My accountant once

Creative Meditation

If you have a regular meditation practice—or would like to begin one—you might want to devote part of it to expanding the internal space you give to your creativity. On a low table in front of your meditation area, arrange objects that represent your creative work: a jar of well-used paintbrushes, a bowl of thread and fibers, something you've created, such as a small sculp-ture or a framed drawing—something pleasing to your eye and associated with creative energy. Set candles on either side and light them before you begin your meditation, taking a few moments to gaze at the arrangement of art and light and let its energy infuse your practice.

and shapes were so beautiful, and we learned everything about lichen—home schooling in action! This got me thinking about recreating lichen in art, and I experiment-ed with a number of new materials in this process. This led to my painting on cotton batting and stitching it into a 3-D lichen. My quilt *Graven Images* was inspired by old New England grave stones after visiting cemeteries where our ancestors were buried.

"People always ask how long a piece took to make. Should I begin counting when that first glimmer of an

said that he thought I had too much time on my hands because I drew drawings for the cover of the notebook of tax information that I gave him. But the truth is, I just try to make everything an art project, fun and different; and that applies to doing taxes or whatever. If I have to do it, I want it to be done fun, right, and in a creative place both physically and in my mind. That's why I have a little hula girl stuck on my adding machine, and I like using an old 1940s Art Metal Inc. desk to do my accounting. And if I am doing accounting, I want to be able to look over the top of my monitor once in a while and see some art on the wall, or a funky old lamp."

Traci says, "My work and ideas are a constant thing in my interior space. It's hard to turn off the switch, which I guess is a good thing most of the time. I think about my art and projects every day, even if I'm not able to paint or do artwork. I usually have ideas in the middle of the night, so I write those down, too. I think it's important to always have space for creativity inside. I wouldn't be the same person if I didn't have those thoughts." Other artists mentioned this, too—the sense that their art, and their thinking about their art, is who they are.

Lisa concurs, saying, "I think one of the things people have a hard time understanding is that artists live life through their art. It is not something they do; it is what they are. If you can get to the point in your life and work where you can live your art, you are truly blessed."

Roz says, "I would say that my art inhabits almost all of my interior space. I always have my journal with me and am always working in it. If for some reason I'm

Journal Page—Judy Wise

not working in the physical journal, I'm always thinking about ideas and projects, which, as soon as I get over to the journal, get recorded. I have to have this stuff constantly moved out of my brain to make room for the new stuff because there are new deliveries every minute."

Studio—Teesha Moore

It's not always easy, of course. Sometimes your brain obsesses about art, and sometimes it likes to toss in other obsessions, just to see if you're paying attention.

Roz explains, "I do let bills and taxes and daily life intrude. I wish I didn't, and I'm a lot better than I was; but I still do to some extent. What has changed over the past twenty years is that the intrusion is of shorter duration. I can turn off that intrusion very quickly. I've learned to let go of things I can't do anything about. I've learned to stop worrying, take action on things I can do something about, and then get back to my work."

Judy Wise says, "I think about my work all the time, but my mind is a many-chambered mansion: There's plenty of room for family, sex, cupcakes, travel, girlfriends, worry, and dental work. I like to obsess about getting old, going broke, global warming, man's inhumanity to man—all the usual stuff everyone who is sane worries about. But my art, well, that's my spiritual connection, my wisdom, and my gift. In many ways it is everything."

You may be arguing here that you need to reserve some of your brain space for your other work; but keep in mind that many jobs require only a fraction of your brain, and even really demanding tasks require using large amounts of brain space for only part of the time.

Theo tells about what it feels like to give creativity unlimited space in your mind—and in your life. "I feel like my whole entire life is one big creative process. In that way, I feel like I'm always working. I like going on

A Little Reminder

When you have an idea about what your brain is doing all day long, you can begin to encourage it to spend its off-hours more creatively. Make a list of ideas in your little notebook—things you want to pursue, color combinations, pages in your journal, projects you're preparing. Set the alarm on your watch or cell phone or computer to go off every hour. When it beeps, notice what you're thinking about, note it in your notebook, and then gently lead your brain to one of the topics on your list. Don't do any heavy thinking at these times; just remind your brain to think about "wire armatures" or "Quinacridone Gold."

Container Heart—Thomas Mann

long 'idea walks' where I just let my thoughts wander. I try to pay attention to my dreams. When I'm at the grocery store, or on the bus, or riding my bike, I try to notice things—overheard words, interesting faces, shapes of clouds, etc. Noticing things is a creative act, and there's inspiration everywhere. So in that way, I do feel like I'm always working. But I try to relax into it, and just have fun with it."

Teesha has much the same experience, and she says, "I am always thinking about stuff—as I wake up, as I go to bed at night, driving, standing in line at the grocery store. It's a never-ending thought process."

Chris says, "I am constantly creating. If I am riding the bus, I am noticing how people are dressed. It's almost as if I do not have control over it—a truly savant state of mind."

When Tom was in theater in college, Thurber was one of his heroes, so he was happy to have him used as an example. As Thurber was always writing, so Tom finds himself always designing, no matter what he's doing. He explains, "Everything influences me in some way. I spent a good bit of time picking up bits of metal ephemera from the fairgrounds this past weekend at Jazz Fest. I can slip into that creative mode anywhere, sometimes much to the chagrin of the folks I'm with." He goes on to explain—quite wonderfully—why this isn't the liability it might seem to some people.

"I see my role here as an artist to be an important one for me and for the people who own and love the work I produce. I sincerely believe that the objects we make as artists have the mission of connecting people to the infinite. I believe also that these objects become a symbol of the energy exchange that we make with the people who connect to them and us. That is why I strive, conscientiously, to imbue everything I make with the most honest creative energy I can—that I do my very best to exercise energetic creative effort in the making of each object. So, like Thurber, I am always making."

Brain Exercises

You know things always work better when they're in good shape: Your legs are better at hiking when you've been riding your bike regularly, and the car runs better after a tune-up. Yeah, yeah—you know that already. And you've probably seen some version of this creative exercise for your brain—but, just like the older-than-dirt chin-up, it's both challenging and surprisingly useful. So get your brain in shape!

Make a list of everyday objects in your notebook. When your creative alarm goes off, shut your eyes and point at one of them. List at least two dozen original and useful ways you could use this object, then cross it off. Add more objects to your list as you think of them. Here are some to start with:

• One of those pedicure toe-separator things

• Mushroom brush

• Screwdriver

• Doorstop

• Brick

• Shoelace

Susan says, "I think creativity has taken over my mind, and I don't pay more attention to the everyday details. The only other thing that plagues my thoughts besides art is paying the bills. The art has to pay the bills, so the two go hand in hand. So I am always having anxiety attacks when bills are due and we are really stretching the bank account. I am always thinking of the next project or how to solve a problem I have come up against in a piece. I can understand James Thurber's experience about living his writing—I am such a visual person that I am continually collecting objects, images and Web sites that trigger an idea. The rest of my life gets the back burner, especially the household cleaning."

Once again, a lot of figuring all this out—this time and space for art thing—is about learning how your brain works and what it needs to be happy and productive. Perhaps you're like a lot of us in that your brain, when left to its own devices, can become, as the excellent writer Anne Lamott says, a bad neighborhood you don't want to go into alone. Left alone with nothing to occupy it, it will begin to gnaw on the terrors of termites and taxes, death and toothlessness and whether or not you remembered to renew your car tags. Filling that interior space with ideas about light and color and texture and mixing tubes of paint is ever so much better.

Kelly says, "When I began painting and had really just discovered the creative life, I remember feeling so much more relaxed about the bills and the laundry and the chores. Those tasks seemed to drop their importance for me—I was always so strict about keeping a clean and tidy house; but then when I allowed the joyful messes of creativity to enter my life, the neat freak inside of me was given permission to relax and chill out a bit. Whatever I'm doing, I'm thinking about color, texture, ideas. For example, if I'm doing the dishes, I might notice how the colors of the dishes are stacked and it might inspire a new color palette for a painting. My life feels so absorbed in creative process and play that I see and notice things that I wouldn't have noticed before."

Carter says, "I like to read a lot of self-help books that focus on the powers of mindfulness and awareness and gratitude. And these books help me focus my mind on the things that matter most to me, rather than getting bogged down in the details of the day to day. Reading these books has helped me find inner peace so that I have more room for creative thoughts and need less mental space for distracting thoughts. I am surrounded by my creativity, and I love it that way. I am always taking in the world around me, noticing color combinations and patterns in the world that I want to use in my jewelry. I am also blessed to be in a relationship with someone who loves beads as much as I do. So it's easy to let the beads consume us!"

Dare to Hope—Kelly Rae Roberts

Being aware of what's going on, staying "in the moment," is difficult for most of us. It's so much easier to remember the past or plan for the future, but neither of those states of mind really helps nurture your creativity. Teesha explains, "Even though I spend a lot of time thinking about things, lately I find myself spending less time thinking about the future. I have never thought about the past. It doesn't interest me in the least. But where I am finding my thoughts lately has been in the 'now.' Granted, Eckhart Tolle has been an influence on my thinking and actions lately, even without me making a conscious effort to. But, looking back, it is always in the now that I come up with the best ideas. Immediately upon waking and when I am journaling and being in the moment. So, I guess I would say that trying to calm your mind from things you have to do or ideas you want to pursue allows you to be present in the moment and allows some of that universal creativity to flow more readily through you. Most of my best ideas pop out of nowhere and literally make me jump out of my seat or jump out of bed. The next moment I am standing there feeling rather idiotic when my brain kicks in and realizes what just happened. But then I remember the idea immediately and get super excited and energized to start working on it right then and there. It's almost as if there is such a creative surge of energy flowing into me that it makes my whole body respond by literally jumping up. I've learned that if an idea does that to me, I'd better listen and take down notes."

The most important thing you can do is to learn to grant your creativity the time and space it needs to flourish. Give it enough room in your head and watch what wonders it will produce.

Chapter 7

Soul Space

Where You Receive Permission to Play

Now that you've made some internal space for your creative life, let's look at some of the ways you can protect it so it doesn't get filled up with worries and to-do lists. How do you nurture that space and fill it with ideas and the excitement of new endeavors? Pam's method of making her to-do list—an exercise in jump-starting her creativity—is an excellent place to start learning creative approaches to everything from the morning commute to planning meals. An even simpler way is to spend more time playing.

One of the things I hear over and over is that people wish they had permission just to play. They want to play—to make stuff without thinking about the results, to try new things, to experiment—without the pressure of rules or goals or time limits—but they feel guilty when they do it, as if they're cheating by doing something that seems to have no purpose. It's tempting to include here a card, a sort of permission slip, that you could cut out and carry in your wallet. It would have your name on it, and it would give you permission to play. If you were caught doodling with markers on the back of the quarterly report, you could pull out your permission slip and say, "See? I have Permission to Play." Same thing if your kids found you down on the floor with their clay, sculpting hands and feet: You could whip out your permission slip and tell them to give you five more minutes.

Lon Chaney—Lisa Lichtenfels

You don't need it, though. As hard as it may be to believe, you were born with the right—the absolute necessity—to play. Needing permission to play is like needing permission to think. Lisa says, "You cannot be creative if your mind isn't free, and an indication that you are not free is thinking you need permission to play."

Judy Wise agrees, saying, "Play is what it's all about. I remember precisely the moment it all made

Carter Seibels

Lisa Gives You Permission

"So, how do you create mental freedom? That can be a real challenge if you have a busy life with many responsibilities. I don't claim to have the answer for everybody, but what has worked for me in the past is to imagine—really imagine and put yourself there—a moment in your childhood when you were totally free. I like to think about being in seventh grade and getting off the school bus on Friday afternoon. Remember how that felt? School is over, and your time is completely your own, and you don't have to worry about anything. Set aside a time, a place, and look forward to it, like you are a kid in school waiting for the bell. And when that time comes, be yourself—your young self. Don't set any goals for that time, don't imagine that you have two hours and you better make a sculpture in that time. Kids don't think that way. Remember that memory is in you, and it is real. If you can hold on to it, you will be free."

sense to me. The moment I looked at two related works and saw that one was relaxed and impromptu, and the other was perfect but strained looking. One artist was playing, and I love that piece. The other artist was working, and while the result was 'correct,' it brought me no joy. In my own work, I liken this to being self-conscious. When I am self-conscious, I am never bold or daring. I play it safe, and I try too hard. I think it applies to writing, music, painting, most all of the expressive arts. For artists with busy lives, it is somewhat of a challenge to allow ourselves to putter and play, but it is also imperative that we do so."

Carter says, "As adults, I think we forget that play is important. As an artist, I am always 'working'—whether I am actually sitting at the torch making beads or not. The mind is always drinking in the world around me and processing, looking for new color patterns, new jewelry constructions, new bead ideas. It's important to give one's self time to develop new ideas on a subconscious level and let things work their way to the forefront, and I

Italy Journal—Kelly Rae Roberts

A Tip from Judy Coates Perez

"Make a play-date with a group of fellow creative spirits. Take time to laugh and talk while working in another medium using tools or materials you do not normally work with."

think play is an important part of that process. It frees the mind and soul. So many times I have found that new ideas or new directions come from playing in other mediums or allowing myself time to do things that I love that don't seem to be directly related to what I do—making beads. I dabbled in lots of mediums last year—PMC (precious metal clay) and resin were two that I really enjoyed. Now after playing with these new-to-me techniques, I came back around to my own glass work and incorporated some of the PMC and resin techniques into my glass and came up with an entirely new line of glass beads. All as a direct result from playing freely with other mediums."

Chris agrees about the importance of exploring, and he adds, "I love to try new stuff to add to my sculptures. I just took a class in glass casting, and I would like to add all kinds of glass shapes to the dolls that I'm creating now. I'm always looking for something new to try, looking for a new way to work the clay or experimenting with different kinds of fabrics and fibers." You don't have to take a class with the intent to learn something new to add to your work. You *can* do that, but it's just as valid to take the class with no idea that you'll ever be able to use glass casting at all. You take it because it sounds like—*gasp!*—fun. You want to play with glass, and that's enough. If it turns out that the techniques you learn are perfect for making some new component for your work, great. If not, also great: You have fun, you get to play, you learn something new, which your brain always appreciates. Your brain likes new stuff.

Pam's Tips

- Try setting a time limit for yourself. Say you are going to just play for thirty minutes or an hour or two. That way you don't feel like you end up "wasting" the whole day.

- Tell yourself if you do some unpleasant task that you've been avoiding, like making an appointment at the dentist or balancing your checkbook, your reward will be a play time—kind of like a recess. Then you get to feel good about getting that one thing done that you've been avoiding, and getting the play time. Win-win.

- Figure out how to assign yourself a task that will require you to play. Like volunteer to design a flyer for your church group or office party. Then use that as an opportunity to experiment with a new set of paints or new computer program. Again, win-win: You get to play and feel good about helping out.

- Start a blog. You'll feel like you need to play to have some material to write about.

Lori's Story

"I'd been really busy planning my first fashion show. I'm a stickler for details, so I'd spent hours, days, weeks, gathering a creative team, putting together press packets, designing the show program, and planning every aspect of the event. Right in the middle of this, a friend came by for a visit.

"We poured a cup of strong coffee, grabbed a couple of giant chocolate-covered cookies, and went up into my work space. I was in the early stages of designing the final look—a wedding dress—and she asked that I continue to work while she hung out, tried on clothes, etc. She threw out a couple ideas about the dress, which I filed away in my brain; and once we really got to talking, I ceased working on the project while we visited.

"We started pulling out some of my raw materials—the salvaged garments that I design my clothes from—and she became my living, breathing mannequin while we mixed and matched the pieces. She whirled and twirled like the ballerina in a vintage jewelry box as I layered a pink silk chiffon skirt with an ivory and pink floral shirt, and we went into my workroom to find just the right striped celluloid button to place at the empire waistline. Next, she served as my personal stylist and chose the outfit for me to wear to the show, much improving on my original idea. When she left for the day, I realized that our 'fun' had inspired some changes to the wedding gown, which took me in an entirely different direction with the design." In this case, playing with a friend was exactly the spark Lori's brain needed to generate a new idea. Your brain needs play too; it helps keep that creative space full of ideas.

Skating on Thin Ice—Pam RuBert

Kelly Rae says, "There's nothing more fun than to go to your favorite craft or art store and come home with goodies. New paint colors to try, the latest scrap papers to play with, new glitter and sparkly embellishments. I love to put all the pressure of creating a masterpiece aside and simply play with all the stuff in the studio—it's how we give ourselves permission to experiment and push the bounds of our creativity. In the end it's the playful experimenting that comes through in our actual masterpieces! So yes, I'm all about playing. What I find happening is this: The more I play and experiment with my supplies, the more relaxed I become. The pressure slips away, and I'm simply in the moment having fun. After all, if I'm just messing around, then I can't really make any big mistakes, right? There's no wrong or right when you're experimenting. Instead we enjoy the process of creating so much

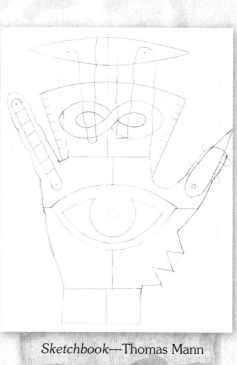

Sketchbook—Thomas Mann

more. We learn new things, and our creative spirit soars when we give ourselves the freedom and permission to simply play and have fun. It's just you, your paints and the freedom to experiment and get messy with all your favorite supplies! All of this relaxation and spirit of play transfers when we're actually not really experimenting anymore but perhaps creating more polished works. In the end, it all feels like play, and this is exactly how it should feel: It's our creative spirit rising and rejoicing as it's being released and having fun!"

Judy Perez, too, knows that little frisson of joy over a brand-new set of paints or threads or paper. She says, "Ooh, there is nothing better than pulling out a new art supply to experiment with. Play is crucial to creativity and generating new ideas."

For Roz, play tends to be a little more structured, but that's because that's how Roz's brain likes to play. She says, "I don't know if I can even define play properly. I always seem to have been a workaholic, but my work seems very playful to other folks, and to me, too, since I love solving visual and organizational problems."

More Little Hints

Some of the other hits of inspiration mentioned by our artists include:

- Pam: "My husband and I often take trips, and our trips are always about art—either to an art event, show, installations, or to visit some other artists. That's what we do: travel to see art and artists."

- Lisa: "I think artists need to see the work of other artists, writers—see movies, go to museums, go to a play on occasion. Nothing makes a person feel more alive than experiencing something excellently done. I am very grateful for all the creative people doing fantastic work. Also I am very lucky to live with a poet. We can influence each other without stepping on toes—I love to see him perform his poetry."

- Kelly Rae: "I also recharge my creative soul through community—by attending art retreats and meeting other creative souls just like me—people I can connect with again online, through e-mail or through blogging. The spirit of creative community really moves me and gets my creative spirit happy with joy."

Theo and His Creative Brain

Theo fills his creative space with his own imagination, keeping himself entertained and sparking ideas for drawings no matter where he is. He explains:

"I try to do a lot of silly, playful things inside of my own head, just to keep my imagination exercised and to keep me from becoming too serious. When I'd have to run all over town doing chores, I began to notice how heavy and serious I would begin to feel. So I started doing something that I call invisible performance art. While riding the bus home at night, I would envision the inside of the bus being overgrown with trees and funny creatures singing in the branches. While waiting in a painfully slow line at the post office, I would imagine the room filling up with water, and impossible sea creatures swimming between and around my fellow line-waiters. Sometimes when I'm walking down the street, I like to pretend I have an invisible stunt-double that runs straight up buildings, back flips over cars and does other daring feats, while I walk calmly down the street. I like to pretend that I have an invisible third arm that can reach all the way to the horizon and touch distant mountains, pet the sunset and lift up the roofs of houses. Imaginary performance art is my personal way of making sure my imagination stays awake and alive through all the mind-numbing but necessary activities I need to do to remain a responsible human being."

Stitching Sample—Pam RuBert

And as for my personal artwork, well, the case can be made that all I do is play. Isn't play about having a joy in experiencing something on a whim and seeing where it goes? I believe that if I throw myself into a creative work situation, then the muse will come, and stay a long, long time. So for me, play is creating a situation where that can happen. I may be engaged in things that seem like work to other folks, but because my mind is engaged in the discovery of something, I'm happy and approaching it in a playful fashion. Great things come out of it."

Pam believes absolutely in the importance of play. She says, "Look at most of the innovative companies that stay ahead of the curve—they have an emphasis on re-search and development. That's what I think play is to the artist, in a way—an investment in the future. You may not see the rewards that day or week or year; but in the end, I believe it will lead to your growth as an artist and free

your mind to be more relaxed and creative in general."

There are other ways to fill that creative space, too. Judy Perez says, "I think having a group of kindred creative spirits is a fabulous way to get recharged and pushed creatively. There is so much to be learned in a small supportive group. When I lived in Austin, several other women and I formed a group with a focus on art quilts. We met regularly in each others' homes and shared our work. On these days we dyed, painted and marbled fabric, worked with clay, carved stamps, painted ceramic tiles, shared our personal stories, supported one another, and cheered each other on."

Some artists firmly believe in scheduling art dates, à la Julia Cameron's *The Artist's Way*. Whatever you call them, these appointments for getting out and exposing yourself to inspiration are a big help in maintaining that creative space in your brain.

Lori says, "That book had a great influence on me when I read it about ten years ago. It helped me to start thinking of myself as an artist. I also wrote 'morning pages'—three or four pages of longhand in that stream-of-consciousness style. I still have stacks of those spiral notebooks that were a part of my everyday experience. I love going back and just opening up to any page and being able to relive that day." These days when Lori needs a hit of inspiration, she heads into the city.

"I am inspired visually so I really enjoy a solid afternoon of people-watching in a large urban setting, taking in the street fashion, graffiti, shop windows, etc." One of these days she and Traci are bound to run into each other, since Traci is out there, finding inspiration in many

Journal—Teesha Moore

of the same places. She's the one, re-member, who's zipping through life—and multiple time zones—on about five hours of sleep a night. She says, "When I need to slow down and nurture my creative spirit, I like to make a cup of tea and listen to music. For inspiration, I like to go to vintage or thrift stores, indie designer bou-tiques and used bookstores. I always have my camera with me, so I take photos everywhere I go. I take photo journals of interesting signs and text I see, writing and graffiti, textures. . . ."

Turns out that little digital camera is a huge boon to creativity. Lots of artists carry one everywhere, tak-ing photographs of things the rest of the world never notices—puddles, gum wrappers, peeling paint. The very act of taking the photos will lead you into that creative space where you look at things like piles of rusted metal

have a live community of creative souls, the virtual community of the Internet can sometimes provide just the creative encouragement needed. Pam says, "About three years ago, I started a blog. The blog and the Internet have been a great boon to me. I love being able to subscribe to other artists' blogs so that drawings and photos pop right into my e-mail box every day. It takes time to manage the technology, but it's worth it for me."

For many artists, there's one thing that's more important in the support of your interior creative space than every-

Making Your Own Journal

Making your own journals is immensely satisfying. Roz and Judy and Teesha all make their books from paper they love, bound in a way that works for the way they use their individual journals. Roz says, "My visual journals are books that I make myself, using artist papers that I enjoy working on, making books sized in formats that I enjoy working in. It is great fun for me to make my own books, and I've devised a method of case binding that is quick and sturdy—dubbed The Roz Method by a friend—that allows me to really use the book in the field but still have an elegant and delightful book. My main goal is to fill my books with the things that catch my interest, or my thoughts, or my sketches. Making my own books, using the paper I love to work on, is sheer pleasure for me."

Journal—Teesha Moore

and see an idea for sculpting jewelry. Kelly Rae says, "I carry my camera everywhere I go and take photos of whatever is calling me to see it. It might be the color of a flower I've never noticed before, or it might be my cute yellow shoes I'm wearing today. Taking photos gives me the opportunity to find the sacred in the ordinary, which allows my creative spirit to soar."

She adds, "I also love keeping a blog—a space where I can spill the content of my heart, especially when it comes to living the creative life." For those who don't

thing else put together: the journal. The sketchbook. That ratty old notebook you carry around with you everywhere. If you don't keep a journal, you might find the emphasis on it a little puzzling: What's the big deal about carrying around a notebook and scribbling things in it all the time? But if you've gotten into the habit and have found it works for you, nurturing your creativity in amazing ways, you're a total convert. No matter where you are, you have that concrete connection with your interior space, with your interior creative life. If you feel bored, you can open it up and sketch or write or doodle. If you feel lonely, you can go back and read the things you've written or chuckle over things you've drawn. If you're stumped for an idea, why, what better inspiration than page after page of notes about projects you wanted to try out when you had just a little more time?

Susan says, "I have sketchbooks at home and at the studio just in case I have an idea that I want to record. I write down class ideas and jot down notes about projects I am working on."

Carter says, "I have a journal that I write in every morning, and I've been doing this since I was in sixth grade—on and off, but mostly on. Though I am a visually stimulated person, my journal is almost all writing

Keeping Track

Roz explains how she uses her journals in her work: "I index them when I'm finished. I go through about eighteen to twenty-two journals a year. When I finish each one I number the pages and index it using a form I made in File Maker Pro. This allows me to sort by subject. The advantage to this system is that, if I'm asked to paint an eagle or a beagle, I can search the keywords and find all the images I've made of that topic or subject and use them for reference. If I want to find a tear-down diagram for a book structure I created, I can search the index and find all my notes from that project and have everything I need to quickly prepare a handout and teach a class on it or make that book another time."

Roz's Journaling Tips

Roz teaches visual journaling classes, and here's what she always tells her students:
- Carry your journal with you everywhere.

- If you don't already have a daily journal habit, work into one with something like fifteen minutes a day.

- Don't wait to have a huge journaling session on the weekend. You won't do it, and it will seem like a chore. And you'll forget half the things you wanted to write about and sketch.

- In the same vein, don't try to play catch-up. If the moment has passed, let it go—work in the moment, or you'll miss the life you're having.

- Don't try to make perfect pages. The journal is about practice, growth, exploration.

- Write and draw for yourself as the audience.

- Use all of your senses in describing things—these little details matter when you look back on an entry.

july 20. 2006   9 p.m.
3 Lake Rocks I found
at Paradise Beach the other
day when Jack was here.
Jack was here before I got here
and stayed last night. This morning
he made us 10 grain Blueberry
pancakes and took off for the
Twin cities around 9 a.m.

There are thin veins of white in the above
large rock.

July 20. 2006   9:20 p.m.
A Lake Superior rock Art
brought over from the mantel.
It was going well but the announcer
for the Tour de France kept saying
"Tour day France" and I started
to laugh while working over the
deep hole. This paper won't take
anymore work so I'll just splatter
on the white specs.

This rock had a slight brownish tinge
except in the hole where it is very
gray and then a mineral center.

(Bob Rolls is the announcer.)

Journal—Roz Stendahl

Why Do You Journal

Roz tells her students, "Ask yourself why you want to journal. What purpose is the journal going to serve? Do you want to create artists' books instead? After you have looked closely at the motivation and desire you have about journals, then you can create a book that really serves those purposes and goals for you. Keeping that type of journal will be easy because it matches the desires you have. And you can always reassess what is working and what isn't." Take a few minutes and think about this, making some notes about the ways you'd like a journal to work for you.

because I get frustrated with my drawing skills. I don't really write about anything 'creative,' but I use my journal more as a place where I can let go of the day. I work through things that are weighing on me, I write about the things going on in my life, so that my mind is freed up for more creative thoughts. I do have one journal that I use to jot down ideas that I have for jewelry, and sometimes I sketch things out here."

Traci says, "If I wake up thinking about ideas, I make sure to jot them down. I keep my journal notebook right next to my bed just for this purpose. I usually make notes right before I go to sleep to remind me what I have to accomplish when I wake up in the morning. My notebook is always with me, so if I have ideas or want to write notes, I can pull it right out of my bag."

Traci Bautista

Teesha, whose own journals were instrumental in spurring the huge interest in art journaling, is one of our avid journal keepers. She believes completely in the power of the journal to transform lives in positive ways. She says, "Journaling is something that always calls me back when I have put it to the side for a little while. It whispers my name and reminds me of the joys of getting lost in the process. It entices me back to it like a lover. The journal is the most direct path for me to nurture my creative soul. Your creative energy wants and needs to come out, and it sometimes is stifled when you are creating work to sell or worried that a commissioned piece will not please the customer. Not all art is divinely inspired. But when you get into your journal, everything relaxes around you—your mind, your thoughts, even your methods of making 'perfect' art—it all just melts away and allows the universal creative energy to start flowing through your open channels. This, to me, is like being plugged back in to charge up my soul. That is the reason I so strongly urge artists to keep journals. It is a vital tool that I need to stay energized and excited about making art and coming up with new ideas."

Judy Wise says, "Well, now. The journal. I'm obsessive about writing and always have been.

103

Journal—Roz Stendahl

dialogue, anything and everything. I keep a written journal that never leaves my desk. I write about things that bother me, write about story ideas, write about drafts of stories, respond verbally to things that are bothering or interesting me. I keep a design journal for my computer work. I keep a beading journal for my bead work. Sometimes design work and bead work will creep into the visual journal because I'll be out and about and think of something I can use in design or beading. But typically I keep those subjects segregated for the simple reason that, in design work and beading, I'll burn through lots of paper; and I don't want to eat up the lovely watercolor paper in my visual journal for thumbnails of college textbook design. Also I find it disruptive

I write nearly every day. I say what's on my mind, looking at my life from a generous point of view. My journal is not a book of complaints; it is more a book of thanksgiving and prayer. I talk to myself there, as a kind mother would speak to a child, encouraging, nurturing, forgiving. My own mother has passed, but there is still some of her wisdom inside of me that I can communicate with in my journal. It's rather complicated, but that's part of it. I love to start my day in my journal because that is a place where I am free to doodle and be silly. Once my brain has made the transition from left to right, it is easier for me to move on to more serious work, but in the spirit of play. The pieces I do that disappoint me are always the ones that lack this carefree quality."

Roz, who has kept a journal since before she started elementary school, explains her various journals and their functions: "I keep a visual journal, which is with me all the time. I use it to sketch in and to take notes about projects, project ideas, thumbnail sketches, overheard

Journal Prep

Roz suggests painting and collaging journal pages as you have time. She explains, "I work in my journal all day long, doing backgrounds and such whenever I have a few minutes—waiting for something around the house to finish, or waiting for glue to dry. Then when I take the journal and go out into the world, I have fun backgrounds to work on."

Journal Spread—Judy Wise

to have to search for a beading design amongst other work. Having all the beading stuff in one book is really great for going back and finding the way I solved a certain problem in stitching or something.

"I also have a computer journal that is basically a dialogue between me and the computer tech I use, who is marvelous. This was another one of those mental breakthroughs I made. After years of knowing everything about every computer, I found, coming back from the car accident, that it was burdensome to get back to that level of knowledge. I wanted to use my time for other things. My computer knowledge is still rather large compared to most folks, because of the time I spend working on the computer, but it feels really good to have let go of the control of it all."

Even if you've tried using a journal in the past and weren't captivated by the process, give it another shot, thinking of it this time as a way to make more space for your creative life. Then, once you have your interior creative space established, we'll turn our attention to an exterior space where you can actually go to bring your ideas to life.

105

Chapter 8

Real Space

Where Art Happens

 No matter what you call it, the place you go to make art is important. It need not be big nor fancy, but it must work for you. You might think that working artists—people who earn their living from the art they create—would all have perfectly appointed studios filled with everything they could possibly need—with maybe even maid service and someone to deliver their meals.

Oh, but how wrong you would be! While everyone would love to have The Perfect Studio, whatever that happens to mean to each of us, working artists will tell you that the layout and design of the studio is really not very important in the larger scheme of things. Sure, it's nice to have a place that's conducive to doing your work, but if you're determined to work, you can do it just about anywhere. Listen to Theo.

"Right now I work out of a little spare bedroom in my apartment. It's the most space I've ever had, yet it's

Theo Ellsworth

still not enough; and it's far from ideal. I figure you can't wait for the right situation to come along before you can start being prolific. I lived out of my car through most of my early twenties. My studio was my backpack for a very long time, which is the main reason I got used to working

Chris Malone

so small, and mostly with the most basic art supplies—paper and pen. I've never really had a great art space, but my little rickety drawing table is my magic spaceship!" That's an attitude that's really important if you want to make art. So many of us think that what's holding us back is the lack of a perfect studio. We tell people—and ourselves—that we'll be able to work when we get the spare bedroom cleaned out, or when we convert the garage into a studio or have that little room built out in the backyard. And, sure, if you're welding metal and making 20-foot sculptures, you're not going to be able to do it out of your backpack. But if you're serious about wanting to make art, you can figure out a way to do it in whatever space you have. And we're here to help. One way we can do that is to show you that working artists make their art in every kind

of studio you can imagine, from tiny to huge.

Chris says, "I work out of my home and, at this time, on an island in the kitchen. I have a space in the basement; but for some reason right now I am more comfortable in the kitchen. I start to work in my kitchen, and after a few hours I move into the back garden, and from the back garden I will go to the roof deck. I do not have a designated work space—all of my space is my work space. The other day my partner came back from New York with a magazine in hand, and it was about studio space. I reluctantly looked at it, and I was just in awe of how neat and clean the featured space was; and I knew that if I had this space for three minutes, it would

A Room of Your Own

Kelly Rae Roberts

What kind of space do you need to work in? Pretend for a moment that you can have anything—that money and space are not issues. What would you need? While you might think that a huge space separated from your house would be ideal, it might not be. If you have only an hour or two a day to spend in your studio, is it worth having to commute to get there? Here are some things to think about:

Do home and family obligations require you to be close by? Do you like to work on your projects at random times? If you draw or do handwork in the evenings, would it be a burden to carry projects back and forth to a separate studio?

How much space do you really need? And are you one of those people for whom clutter seems to expand to fill *any* available space? Sometimes a small area that's just big enough is better than a cavernous space just waiting to be filled up.

In your journal, think about your Dream Studio. Sketch a floor plan and list everything you'd want, from the skylight to surround sound to state-of-the-art jeweler's bench. Dream big! List everything! Then go back and circle the most important things—the big windows for natural light, the access to running water.

Now let's be practical. Given the money and space at your disposal, what kind of studio will work for you? First look at areas in your house or apartment: spare rooms, but also unused rooms such as a formal dining room, laundry room (my own studio shares a 10'× 18' space with the washer and dryer), garage, gardening shed. Even a large closet will work—just one large enough for you to install a sturdy surface that will serve as a desk when you open the door and pull up your chair. Go back and look at your Dream Studio list and note the things you circled. Do you need to be near a sink for running water? What kind of light do you need? What about heating and cooling?

108

be in total chaos. I am not a neat, clean, everything-has-its-place person. I wish I were more organized, but I am not."

While basements, in theory, sound like a good idea, you might want to spend some time down there, just sitting and reading a book, before you jump in and convert yours to a studio. Kelly tells about trying to work in her basement. "The worst workspace I ever had was a little area I created for myself in the basement of our home. The basement was totally grungy and dark and uninviting, so of course I rarely went down to my little space. I think it's important that we create spaces that are inviting, a place where you'll actually want to go and play for a bit."

These days, Kelly has moved upstairs, where she's much happier. "My studio is an unused bedroom in our house. It's small but inviting and functional. It has two large windows on one wall and French doors on another—so lots of light. I have a large table where I paint and a great big bookshelf, made from recycled wood scraps, that holds containers full of my supplies—paint, paper, glue, etc. I have another large table that I use for cutting and matting my

Lori Sandstedt

has developed into what I call my Shrine Wall. It's full of all kinds of things that inspire me or that I've collected from my travels and walks. There's some of my own art and postcards from events I've been involved in, friends' art and artists that I love. I've also put all kinds of objects on the wall. There's a turtle shell, an otter skull I found on the beach and a fox skull I found in the forest. There are rocks, shells, dried leaves and flowers, mossy sticks and seed pods—all kinds of things. There's something very satisfying and comforting about this wall. I also have my preschool diploma in a frame that says that I've 'learned how to play and am ready for kindergarten.' I have another worktable with 'zine-making supplies. I have a whole wall of books—mostly graphic novels, comics, art books, and novels. I have a little stereo and all my CDs. I have piles of old frames and lots of old empty ink bottles."

prints, packing my orders and other non-painterly tasks. Under the tables are shipping supplies, surplus inventory of prints and cards, and file cabinets."

Theo, who finally has a Room of His Own, adds, "It feels amazing to have a space that's just for doing art, no matter how small or inadequate the space. It allows me to be that much more focused and prolific. My studio feels kind of like this invisible snail shell that travels with me wherever I go. It's only been able to physically manifest in small ways, but I keep growing out of one space and into a slightly bigger one as time goes on. It's been a long journey from a backpack to a small spare room, and every state has been a different kind of focus for me. I'm actually hoping by the end of the year to be able to rent an art studio somewhere. I like the idea of leaving the house each day and having a bit of a journey between my house and my studio. I want to have my own magic make-believe place that I go to and close the door, clock in and bring dreams into the world all day, clock out and make my journey home. I'm going to call my studio The Thought Cloud Factory. Right now my little spare room is fine. The wall in front of my drawing table

Lori Sandstedt

Lisa Lichtenfels

Lisa Lichtenfels

What's In Your House

Go through your house and make notes about the use of space. Do you have a room that's used only when you have company? Is there a spare bedroom that's serving only as a storage space? What about that closet that's full of clothes nobody has worn since the 1990s? Make notes about all the space and then start thinking how you can claim some of it as your own. It may take some bartering—you give your partner your half of the garage in exchange for the spare bedroom—but there's bound to be at least a few square feet that you can use to set up a studio.

Lori also works at home. She says, "When I first started out and was designing handmade greeting cards, I used the dining room table. I didn't have a dedicated work area at that time, but since we rarely used the dining room, it worked out fine. I do remember having to 'clean up the place' if we had guests. I never liked that everything was out in the middle of the house—I like having a private space that is my own. I have two rooms upstairs, one designated as studio space, the other a guest room upon which I continue to encroach. I use the smaller studio space primarily for designing jewelry and sewing. It houses my button collection, scrap leather, hardware, supplies for jewelry and handbags. My dress form lives in the guest room along with the raw

Judy Coates Perez

materials for fashion—garments waiting their turn to be redesigned, drawers full of silk scarves, fabric remnants, ribbons, trim, etc. My complete garments hang on rolling racks on either side of the bed. Besides all of the 'necessary' supplies, I have a book collection—my favorite is *The Language of Clothes*, by Alison Lurie—a huge mobile I designed from vintage yardsticks and colorful objects, a shelf full of little things that are meaningful to me, a bulletin board covered in quotes about creativity, a little stack of projects that I can work on when I'm not in the mood to sew, a wooden crib railing where I hang fabric remnants, and of course my trusty vintage Bernina. And yes, I value all of these items—they are as much a part of my creative scenery as my creative history."

Lisa, who also works at home, says, "This is the best workspace I have had so far. The worst was the college dorm room. It was cramped, and there was always somebody playing loud music even at night. I love my studio—I can't wait to get in there first thing in the morning. I knew we had to buy this house because I knew I could work here. Having a separate building as a studio would be a dream. I'd love to have three spaces—storage/business, photography and studio. As it is, this one space has to service all three. Because of space considerations, almost everything in my studio is practical. Still, I have found spots for the funky and fun, like skeletons."

Roz Stendahl

Traci seems to have an ideal studio space: She works in most of her house and has the freedom to spread out anywhere. In reality, though, things are a little different.

"My home studio takes over the entire house except for my bedroom, bathroom and kitchen. I work in different areas of the house. My sewing machines are pulled out when I need to work on them. I have a large dining room table—it seats ten—that doubles as a studio table when I cover it with brown kraft paper. I also like working on the floor, so sometimes I cover the floor with a sheet and spread out my paints, inks, tools and journal. I have a bookshelf—I call it an inspiration cube—that houses my huge collections of books, art tools, beads and findings, fabrics, yarns, memorabilia and photos—things that are important to me. And, of course, my little Yorkies, Freedom and trei*trei—my studio wouldn't be complete without them. My home workspace is impor-

tant; but it's rarely in use, since I've been on the road for most of the past few years." The perfect studio arrangement doesn't do you a lot of good if you're never in it, so Traci has learned to adapt.

"On the road, my studio is in hotel rooms, on the airplane, in workshop classrooms, and at friends' and family's houses when I visit. I have learned to work everywhere. My work has become more portable. I paint whenever I can, usually no larger than 12" × 18" when I'm on the road—it's much easier to carry while I'm traveling. The background papers I paint are carried with me though my travels, and I use the pieces to create my journals and collage paintings." Traci's experience proves that, for most of us, there isn't one ideal studio space.

Sometimes all it takes is looking at your living space

in a new way. Who said houses have to have dining rooms and living rooms? Judy Perez says, "Years ago we had a very small house, and my studio was in the breakfast nook off the kitchen. This was my worst space, but it was at a time when my children were babies, and it was hard to have time and space for my art. When we moved to Chicago, we decided to skip the traditional house and buy a loft. This was one of the smartest lifestyle choices we ever made. We no longer have a living and dining room; we have a large open work space with big tables, flat files, shelves, file cabinets and a separate library for all the books that doubles as a family room. There is plenty of space for my daughter and me to sew at the

Susan Sorrell

How Neat Do You Have to Be?

Some people have to have everything in its place before they can sit down to work, and others work best in chaos, with all their tools and supplies right out there where they can reach them. Carter says, "As much as I try to be neat and clean, I realize that I am a cluttered sort of person. When I try to fight that natural clutter, I get out of sorts and things don't flow the way they should. So I've quit trying to fight the clutter, and I let it rule. I let the beads pile up, let the mess accumulate, and I let the creativity flow the way it needs to. If that means I have a cluttered studio, that's what it means!" In short, don't try to force yourself to work in a certain way just because you think that's the way you're supposed to work. Figure out what works for you and go with it.

same time and my son to make his origami creations. We have huge 9-foot windows to let in lots of natural light, making it a great space to work in. Because it is obviously a workspace, I don't feel so bad about the constant disorder that made a regular house so messy. I keep all my necessary supplies in the studio area, with the ones used most often within arm's reach. The materials and supplies that I use less frequently I keep in shelving in our bedroom closet."

Roz is lucky to live in a duplex where she has one floor just for her work areas. She says, "I don't know what the best and worst work spaces would be for me. I really do a great job adapting any space I'm given to working for me. I'm kind of like the Borg: resistance is futile. We live in a duplex and use the entire building, upper and lower. I used to have a lovely room on the

Judy Wise

so I had to clear things away. I just couldn't decide to make books on a whim and do it. Downstairs with all the space that used to be a living room and a dining room, I can keep projects on different tables and move from job to job, table to table. I also have an easel up all the time. I find that I paint much more frequently—my personal painting—and I also find that I make books more frequently. So I would say yes, the space has changed my work. I really like being able to get up and work at any time of the day or night. The downside to having converted so much of our home into my studio is that there aren't any relaxing places in the house except the TV room, but since I'm usually working that doesn't really bother me." Roz's next big project is to get rid of supplies and tools she no longer needs to free up more storage space, proving the adage that things expand to take up any available space.

second floor for my studio, but it was tight as my business expanded. Equipment would end up in other rooms, on other floors, and I was running all around all the time. After a bit of renovation downstairs, I ended up moving into the living room and dining room areas and turning that and the front four-season porch all into my studio. It works really well as it gives me a computer area, filing and storage, a library area, a place for my rubber stamp collection, a drawing table, a desk, a work table, a mail table—pretty much anything I need. I guess my work space is important to me because I run a business from it. Things have to be conducive to being productive, and I feel that this workspace is.

"Having the space has changed how I work because when I was upstairs in one small room, I had all my computer stuff to keep the design business going, and I had a drawing table to work on illustrations; but I didn't really paint as much for the pure pleasure of it because I always kept the room pretty clean and tidy for my main work. Also to make books in the space was a problem,

Away from Home

If you need to work away from home, you've got a lot of options, from having a space built in your backyard, as Teesha did, to renting a space in a building or a room in someone's house. You can share space with other artists—perhaps someone you know has a larger studio space and would like to rent or barter one room. Maybe a friend has a spare bedroom and would be happy to have you use it in exchange for house-sitting during the day when everyone's gone. Think creatively—there are rooms and buildings everywhere that are empty and not being used. Offer to paint and fix up one of them in exchange for a six-month's lease.

Carter Seibels

To Color or Not to Color?

Do you work best in a space filled with your favorite colors, or do you need neutral walls and minimal decoration as a background for your work? While it may seem like a minor detail, it can make a huge difference. Buy a swatch of inexpensive fabric in the color you're considering and hang it on the wall you'll face when sitting at your work table. Give it a week or so to see how it affects your mood and the work you produce.

Teesha Moore

"I did a big reorganization last year that bought me some space, but that's already filled up! Pretty much everything in my studio now is work-related and where I can reach it, or it's art on the walls. I think if I had a bigger space where I could have things set out more, I might have more collections, but probably not. I never liked dusting, and this just removes the need to do that."

Judy Wise also works in a home studio that's kind of taken over much of the house: "It is a 448-square-foot room. In addition, I've commandeered a bedroom for my office and the two-car garage and the hallway and most of my husband's shop. The studio is *very* important to me, but I've worked in terrible conditions, too. I can work on large canvases now, and I have more storage space. I had the best studio ever, ten years ago, when I lived a few towns over and had huge, huge space in several rooms of a one-hundred year old house. I had

Sharing Space

Sometimes it's not possible to have a room of your own or even a closet where you can put your stuff and close the door. If you have to share your space with someone else, make sure that you have an arrangement that guarantees your work will be left undisturbed, whether that means buying a storage bin with a lid for your pots or putting a lock on the cabinet where you store your paintings. It's vital that you have some space, even if it's only one plastic tub, where your work will be left alone.

Carter Seibels

an acid hood and zillions of work tables and a whole room dedicated to framing. That was heaven. I was very productive there." Of her current studio, she says, "All the walls are covered with gee-gaws that I and my friends have made that I find to be friendly and inviting. I like to be reminded of that when I am working. I wish I had room for a big couch. And some pillows."

Then there's Carter. Although she has just one room for her studio in her house, she also has a studio at work, which she finds ideal.

"I am very lucky in that I currently have two studios. When I moved to California, I set up my studio in the office. But I quickly realized that that meant I could only make beads during office hours, or that I had to go to the office during off-hours, and I didn't like being in such a big building by myself after hours. I was used to having a home studio back in South Carolina, so sometimes the vastness of our office felt a bit overwhelming.

"So I realized that one of the guest bedrooms in our house wasn't really being used, and I decided that I could turn that room into a studio. I cleaned out all of the old piles of junk and went to work. First I painted the walls a nice pastel cantaloupe color and the opposing beams a bright tangerine color. It's a tiny little room, so the color really makes me feel like I'm inside a ripe piece of fruit! On the wall I hung pictures that are dear to me, and over the carpet I put a rug that used to be in my grandmother's house. Now this room speaks to me, and it has become my haven. I feel a sense of calm when I walk in the room on a sunny afternoon and see the glow of the colors all around me. Now creativity flows in here. I think

Teesha Moore

the energy in a space affects the outcome of what goes on in a space. I try not to let things just pile up in my studio; if something is in there, it should be in there for a reason. I try to only let things come in if they are going to serve as inspiration or work their way into something creatively. I've learned that if 'foreign' objects come into the studio, they can get in the way fast, so I try to keep them from ever entering the doors."

She lists the things on her work table:

"A Converse high-top shoe that's in the process of being decorated, a few back issues of Sundance catalog, some stickers, some PMC pieces in progress, a bag full of pewter charms that I found in the garage, some dried flower petals that I'm putting in resin, some little plastic containers that have polka dots on them that I got at Michael's, some paintbrushes, some bottles of resin, and some glitter. On my bead-making table, I have several piles of beads that are serving as reminders of designs that I want to work on in the future. And of course lots of piles of the ends of glass rods that I'm not sure what I'm going to do with, but I'm holding on to them. I also have a big bag of fabric scraps and a huge pile of clothes that

Thomas Mann

Thomas Mann

want to be altered. There's a sewing machine under the table that I pull out and an entire Ikea cart full of paints, pens, glitters, glues and so on, for when I get time to play with all of that."

Those are the artists who have studios in their homes. For Teesha, who works with her husband, Tracy, moving the studio just as far as their backyard was the ideal solution. It's out of the house and gives them tons more room, but it's only steps away from home and so much better than the days when she worked at a desk in her bedroom and at the dining room table.

"My studio is five steps from the back door of my house. The space is 22' × 36' with two floors and taller-than-average ceiling heights. It is technically called a 'pole building,' so it has two poles going up through the middle of it, but that allowed us to have a ceiling upstairs that is open to the full pitch of the roof. We hired some-one to come in and Sheetrock the walls and another

person to wire it, and we hired neighbor kids to paint it using paint that was mismatched and purchased for $2 a can. The lower floor is simply cement, and we laid a composition tile floor upstairs in colors like magenta and orange and reds and deep yellows. This studio option was *way* cheaper than selling our house and finding a larger one with a studio, and we like the fact that it is a separate space from the house but still close enough to run in to use the bathroom or get water for our brushes.

"I don't like lots and lots of desks, even though I have space for them. They tend to all get filled. I prefer one desk for paperwork and computer and one desk reserved for art endeavors. I keep these spaces clean, so they are always conducive to using."

And then there are the artists who have studios away from home. Tom's studio is upstairs next to his gallery on Magazine Street in New Orleans. While the building itself is huge, his personal work area is quite small and rather nest-like.

"The jewelry artists spend the bulk of their creative life in a little bubble that surrounds their chair and work-bench. I have mine set up to be ergonomically efficient. I have designed and fabricated special tool holders, a soldering mechanism, a vacuum system, etc., that make this little space so workable that I don't have to get up very often to access other technical capabilities. It's also the entertainment center, with my laptop hooked into the music and sound system and the TV where I listen to and half-watch DVDs of favorite films repeatedly, to the point that I can spout the lines in advance of the actors. So, on a good day, I can climb into that bubble and seal off the world to a certain extent and plug away at the 'work.'

"I have to 'go' to work, even if that means walking out to the little studio shop I have in the shed in the backyard. There has to be a sense of separation from my living space." A lot of people feel that way—that unless they leave their house and go somewhere else, they're not really at work.

Susan has created a studio in a house that used to belong to her grandparents. "I have a small house called the Little House Art Studios. This house is a double-bar-rel shotgun shack that was built in the 1920s. My grand-parents bought it back in 1945 and lived in it until 1965. It was their first house, and they rented it after they built a bigger brick ranch-style house next door to it. It is a very simple house and didn't get redone until I made it into a studio in 2007. We put in air and heat, new windows, repainted the inside—and the bathroom will be remodeled in the future. I painted the walls lavender. The inside has to be a colorful space for me to work and make art.

"I have long tables made from old doors and saw-

Susan Sorrell

horses in three of the rooms. I have a stereo set up so I can listen to music. One room is the workshop room, and there is a big table with chairs. I found the table by a dumpster and knew one day it would be a terrific work table, so it has been stored in my great aunt's workshop. I am bad about dumpster diving and rescuing would-be art supplies. I have one room set up for sewing with a sewing machine and fabric bins. The kitchen is where I

Pam RuBert

do all of my painting and fabric dyeing. And one room is a sort of office/public space where I hang out and read. I have my artwork up on the walls like a mini gallery in case I get any buyers dropping by. I have lots of books on bookshelves, like a mini library. Anything I put into my studio is for inspiration or supplies to make art. I hate to have stuff lying around that has no use.

"I feel like my grandparents are with me when I am in the studio working, and I know my grandmother would have loved seeing art being created there. She was my inspiration for pursuing art in the first place."

Pam wins the prize for Biggest Studio, although that's because she shares one with her husband, who needs much of the space in their former peanut butter factory for his large sculptures. The building is about ten minutes from their house, and it's ideal for the work they do.

"Before that, we had a small house with a small studio in the backyard, but any time my husband was building a sculpture, it took the whole space, and usually was too big for the space; and he had to contract out parts of the work. There was no room for me to make other kinds of art; so I tried working in a spare bedroom or the basement, which was dark and often flooded, or on the dining room table. About ten years ago, we renovated the peanut butter factory to be a sculpture studio with multiple dedicated areas for metal fabrication, wood construction, painting, and finishing. Over the past seven years, I've slowly converted a big long room inside the factory to be my fiber studio and soon hope to set up another adjacent area for mono-printing and dye-painting.

"Having such a large building was a serious commitment of time, energy, and finances, but at the same time has transformed our work and reputation. It's also big enough to have enough room to do some fun stuff, like we put in a tiki bar with a pool table and other vintage games as a place to have art parties."

Pam RuBert

When Disaster Strikes

Fires, floods, tornados—all kinds of disasters can befall a studio. In 2007, Pam's studio flooded horribly during an ice storm when the sprinkler system froze and a water main broke.

"All the front offices were flooded, destroying many computers, furniture, files, photos, books, paper supplies, and other equipment. For the last year and a half, we have been consumed with the renovation and replacement of equipment and major parts of the building, including roof, ceiling, walls, and flooring. So

between that and trying to deal with all the paperwork and reconstruction of data, not as much art has been made. During reconstruction, we moved our offices into the tiki bar, and I tried to keep a sense of humor by doing things like storing paper clips and supplies in popo platters, putting the hula girl on my adding machine, etc. But really it's been hard, and I have to admit over the past year, there were times when we felt like giving it all up. But we stuck with it and have taken the opportunity to

Kelly Rae Roberts

rethink and improve the organization of our space and work-flow, to improve our presentation space and add a new gallery space. We're calling it Studio 2.0 because it is definitely new and improved in many ways.

"I'm always trying to build my own studio furniture, like I bought the whole video and floral department at a grocery store auction for $200 and got a whole wall of shelves with glass doors and pink Formica countertops. I took the glass doors off and made them into glass shelves balanced on glass blocks; I used the Formica shelves for my fabric collection. I used pieces of the countertops balanced on some old preschool tables with wooden tops and metal legs—a yard sale find for $40 for four tables—to make a couple of sewing desks." She

says she still has a lot of the grocery store pieces in the back warehouse and will periodically go "shopping" back there to see what else she can find for her studio.

No matter what kind of space you find for your own studio, whether it's a corner of the den or an unused closet or a former snack food factory, you can make it into a space that works for you. Pam leaves you with one little caution, however: "But be warned! If you take the forlorn space and work on it, you will naturally transform it with your presence, your art, and your interesting supplies; and suddenly it will start to look attractive to someone else. So be prepared to defend your space because you made it what it is—don't give it up!"

Now that you've got your space, turn to the next chapter to read about some of the ways you can get its energy flowing around you.

Teesha Moore

Chapter 9

Creative Habits

Music, Candles and Companionable Cats

It's a wonderful thing, indeed, to have an art space all your very own, whether it's a studio straight out of *Where Women Create* by Jo Packham, or a rickety little card table set up next to the bird feeder on the back porch. It doesn't matter what the space is like; it only matters what you're like when you're there. Are you inspired? Excited to get to work? Sometimes you can walk into your studio and immediately be filled with ideas and energy. Other times? Well, other times you may need a little help.

That's where little studio rituals come in. Now, when I ask artists if they have any rituals in their studios, they tend to look at me blankly, as if I'm asking about chanting and the sacrifice of small animals. That's not it at all, of course. Most artists don't have any formal rituals, but when you begin talking to them about their routine and habits and the things they do when they flip on the light and tie on their studio apron, well . . . that's another thing entirely. Listen to Traci, for example. She says, "I don't have any routines while I'm in my studio, but I enjoy listening to music while I work . . . I sometimes light candles and definitely always have food and drinks handy. I also enjoy tea when I am relaxing and taking a break in my studio chair."

Chris Malone

Studio Teas

I asked our tea-drinking artists for their personal recommendations. If, like me, you've never really bonded with tea, you might find one here that you love—or at least one that you know is being savored by one of your favorite artists.

Carter:
- African Nectar (red herbal and flower tea) by Mighty Leaf (www.mightyleaf.com)
- Chamomile Citrus (also by Mighty Leaf)
- Hibiscus tea (iced)
- Chai tea

Judy Perez:
- Earl Grey and English Breakfast with cream (during the day)
- Herbal Vanilla Hazelnut (in the evening)

Judy Wise:
- Haarlem Honeybush by Honest Tea (no caffeine)
- Jasmine Pearls Green Tea (by Tao of Tea)
- Rose Petal Black Tea (by Tao of Tea)
- Malty Assam Tea (black tea by Tao of Tea)

Kelly Rae:
- Tazo Awake black tea with milk and sugar
- Tazo Green Ginger tea
- Tazo Vanilla Apricot white tea

Susan:
- Green tea with chai tea, iced
- Celestial Seasonings and Tazo teas (various ones throughout the day)

Teesha:
- Market Spice Tea, iced (Pike Place Market in Seattle)
- Matcha green tea

Traci:
- Homemade ginger tea (see recipe on page 126)
- Mighty Leaf Green Tea Tropical
- Organic Lemongrass and Ginger loose-leaf tea (T2, Australia)
- Tazo Zen tea
- Teavana Emerald Princess Green Tea
- Teavana Too Life White Tea
- Numi Flowering loose teas ("Beautiful to look at in the tea pot.")

And for those of us who just don't do tea? Chris says, "I have got to be honest. I don't drink teas unless I'm not feeling well. But I do love a Jack and coke and a nice cigar around 1:30PM. I find that this helps to break up the day . . . this is what I tell myself."

Tea Tips

Here are a few tea tips to help you on your adventures in trying new studio teas.

Judy Perez says, "Usually, I make one cup of tea at a time, since it invariably goes cold while I am working if I make more. I also have the benefit of a water cooler that has hot water, so I don't even need to boil the water. I do have the ritual of liking to drink my tea out of a particular cup. It's a cup I picked out for my birthday several years ago from a potter in northern California. During the winter I like to drink tea all day long, so I might switch to a decaf or an herbal tea late in the afternoon."

Teesha says, "My way with tea: Take the time in the morning to boil some water. Fill a thermos up with water and herbal tea bags—herbal tea is like drinking medicine for what ails you. Carry it with you wherever you go. *Voilá!* Instant hot tea throughout the day and into the evening if you have a good thermos. I know a few different artists whom I never catch without their thermos with them. In fact, I believe in this so much, I gave all the Artfest attendees a thermos last year in their goody bag—with the Artfest logo on it, of course.

"If I need to increase my mental clarity in the afternoon, I will whip me up some matcha green tea powder with a little soy milk, molasses, and ice."

Susan recommends, "I like to drink green tea with chai tea, iced:
3 green tea bags
2 chai tea bags
Boil water and let sit for 7 minutes.
Mix with water in a pitcher
This gives you enough iced tea for a few days. Also, I sweeten it with the natural sweetener, Stevia."

Kissed on Both Cheeks—Kelly Rae Roberts

For Traci, it's ginger tea that does the trick. "This is served everywhere in Bali, and I love it:
½ cup coarsely chopped fresh ginger root (don't bother peeling it, but give it a quick rinse before chopping)
3 cups of water
honey to taste
In a small saucepan, combine the ginger root and water, bring to a boil and simmer for ten minutes. Taste, and if it tastes too weak, continue simmering; if it tastes too strong, add more water. Strain and sweeten with honey. And a squeeze of lemon, too—yummy!"

And there's Chris, who's come up out of his basement studio and is working at the island in the kitchen. He says, "I like to keep incense burning in the back garden all day as I work. After I take care of the garden, birds and dogs—this can take up to three hours—I will have a yogurt and a glass of juice or something and put on some music. On other days I might play a movie like *Revenge of the Pink Panther*. Who knows? Whatever I feel on that day."

Studio rituals are less what you think of as capital-R "Ritual" and more about routine, habit, the little things that get you going.

Judy Wise has sort of no-ritual rituals. When I ask her if there's anything she does to prepare for the day, she says, "Yes: eating! That's my main routine. No rituals like sharpening pencils. Keep the chips and diet pop flowing and keep the music on. I have to have all my comforts close at hand. I just like to be surrounded by the clutter of collage paper and my paints—then I can usually get right to it."

Judy Perez says, "If I am going to be working in a methodical manner painting or free motion quilting, I really enjoy listening to audio books. So if I do have a habit or ritual, it might be to make sure I have a good audio book lined up, and a cup of tea."

By now you've probably noticed that quite a few of our artists talk about tea as a studio staple. Check out *Studio Teas* on page 125 for more information about some teas you might want to try in your own studio.

For some of us, the day doesn't start until the coffee's on. Susan says, "When I get to my studio, the first thing I do is turn on the coffee. I have it already made up, ready to go before I leave each day, so all I have to do is turn it on when I get in. Then I turn on my music, light my candles and put out my house flag—that is to let everyone know I am there if they want to drop in. I turn on my cell phone, since I don't have a landline at the studio. I always have a candle burning, and my usual scent is vanilla—vanilla is a soothing smell to me

Journal—Judy Wise

and makes a place feel cozy. I go around and open all of the window blinds in the house so it is flooded with light. Sunlight is really important to me. If it is nice outside, I will sit on the front porch and drink my coffee during the day on my breaks. Also, the dog comes to the studio with me. Whoopi Doodle is my constant companion."

Your studio space needs to satisfy all your senses, whether you like things completely quiet with no odors or you want rock and roll and a little patchouli. One of the biggest issues for artists at work is sound, whether it's music you choose or the ambient sounds of the neighborhood. Some people prefer music, and some have to work in total silence. Kelly always has music going in her studio. She says, "The minute the music comes on, my creative spirit relaxes a bit, and I get into the mood to paint. Sometimes it's loud rock music, and sometimes it's quiet soothing music. It's hard for me to create without music playing in the background. I also have a favorite

candle that I often have lit when I'm in the studio. And I almost always have a cup of hot tea nearby. It's very, very hard for me to get started without a cup of hot tea."

Carter says, "I almost always have music on. I usually will burn a candle while I'm working, as well, or some essential oils. I love smells, and they really help me focus on the task at hand.

"I tend to get really thirsty when I'm working at the torch, too, so I always have a big bottle of water next to

Now Playing

Music is such an individual thing. Some artists like it mellow, and some want it to rev them up. Here are some of our favorites:

Carter: Something fairly mellow: Van Morrison, Tracy Chapman, Gotan Project, Mark Knopfler, Jack Johnson. Or reggae: Bob Marley, Toots and the Maytals, Taj Mahal.

Susan: Something upbeat, usually disco or dance mixes.

Roz: Mostly silence, but sometimes Gregorian Chants or R. Carlos Nakai playing Native American flute.

Teesha: Zero One, Amethystium, Bluetech, Conjure One, Desert Dwellers, Dido, Earth Trybe, Enigma, Flunk, Higher Intelligence Agency, Kruder & Dorfmeister, Magic Sound Fabric, Omnimotion, The Orb, Phutureprimitive,

Thievery Corporation, Tosca, Waterbone, Zingora. "An iPod with these bands can put you into a twenty-hour, blissful, creative trance that will take you out of this world and into the next. This is always the music that gets me into the creative mode quicker than anything. I *adore* this type of music, but the above listed are my favorites."

Chris: "Prince, classic Motown, Afro-Cuban, some good sweet jazz—so sweet you can taste it, like Charlie 'Yardbird' Parker, or some kind of new-age sounds. Now, the Prince must be pre–1999 or it just won't work out. On other days I might put on some Billie Holiday or Andreas Vollenweider."

Pam: "For active work like cutting out fabric, I like music with a sense of humor or energy: Barenaked Ladies, The Doors, U2, Talking Heads, Komeda, Sea and Cake, The Clash, B52s, White Stripes, Beck. For drawing and quilting, which are more meditative, I like hypnotic music: Thievery Corporation, Bent, Lemon Jelly, Moby, Suba, Bonobo, Diemtre in Paris."

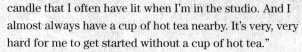

128

me that I drink really quickly. Usually I have some hot herbal tea that I keep refilling as well. If it's night time and I'm working at home, I might have a glass of wine or a beer while I work.

"I usually make at least twelve beads at a time before I get up, because that's the number of mandrels I can fit in my mandrel holder. When I first sit down at the torch, a lot of times I will think of something else that I need to do, something that I've forgotten. The tendency is to jump up and do it right away, but I know that I get easily distracted. So I will make myself make at least one 'set' of beads before I'll let anything distract me. I find that once I get my rhythm, I don't let those distractions even be in the way, and I am in the flow of things."

Teesha says she has "no habits to speak of. I think the simple act of going up the stairs to the studio tells me it's time to get to work on whatever is on my plate for that day. I always like having water close by and try to keep a large water bottle filled with ice water. I fill it every time I go downstairs and into the house to use the bathroom. I do not like eating in my studio. I feel like eating should be done while being fully present. I do, however, like to have a comfy chair in my studio or somewhere private for reading and looking at books or sitting and taking notes." For Teesha, habits are more about the things she doesn't do in her studio—she doesn't answer the phone or take faxes or have people drop by while she's working, and she takes care of

Carter Seibels

e-mails only every other day. Lisa does the same thing. She says the computer is "a lovely thing, but if it starts calling to you too much, you have to set limits." Since it's vital for her to be uninterrupted in her studio, she says, "When I found myself spending too much time with it, I started turning it on every other day. That broke the cycle of addiction." The one exception she makes to interruptions in the studio is making time for a special daily guest.

"I have a routine in the mornings to gently start my day. Normally cats and nylon-fabric sculpture don't mix, but my cat, Fleffnor, has somehow figured it out and does not ever jump on the work surfaces; so as I am doing my work list, I will play a little with her, or maybe she will sit on my lap. When the work begins, I open the door and let my guest out."

Theo also spends part of his day with a cat lying in his lap. "My cat hangs out with me a lot, which is great, except he likes to do sneak attacks on me when I'm carefully inking a detailed picture. I like it when he hangs out and falls asleep on my lap while I draw. Drawing with a sleeping cat on your lap, with a fresh pot of green tea, is pure joy. It's nice to have things to snack on, too, because otherwise I'll get really focused on my project

129

and forget to eat.

"I have a full-spectrum bulb in my desk lamp, which has helped me in a huge way. I like to alternate between music and silence, and occasionally I'll listen to NPR if I need to listen to talking or get tuned in to the happenings in the world. I can usually only do that if I have a lot of pages to ink; otherwise I like to have my own flow of thoughts. I keep my cell phone on vibrate and ignore it unless absolutely necessary. No computer. There's nowhere to sit, except at my drawing table. I wouldn't mind having a cozy place to sit; there's just no room in there."

For Tom, whose degree is in technical theater, set design and lighting, the quality of light in his studio is key. "The lighting has got to be right to make me feel 'at home.' I'm very geared to the

Sounds or Silence

Do you work better with some music in your ear, or do you need complete silence when you're at your most creative? If you're like a lot of artists, you'll find that some tasks go better with music, and some—usually the ones that require more focused, intense concentration—demand silence. For a week, play a completely different kind of music each day—classical on Monday, perhaps; blues on Tuesday, etc.—and make notes about how it affects your work.

Thomas Mann

creation of inspiring environments, and lighting has a lot to do with that." He also likes to keep something to drink close at hand while he's working.

"Seems like I have to have that cup of coffee, or iced coffee when I'm in New Orleans, or a little snifter of brandy or a cup of Earl Grey tea just down the bench for that little break in the action. That small retreat from the work, a little moment for reflection that the beverage provides." Like a lot of people who are constantly on the go, traveling and shifting time zones and working at all hours, Tom has mastered the art of the power nap.

"Naps are essential. I don't get one every day, but a fifteen-minute power nap makes the difference between going home at 8 or 12. So I built a special black couch for the kitchen in the big studio where those naps take place. I've caught staff doing the same on that couch."

Lori says, "I think that, perhaps, if I had more space, I might think more about creating areas to do other activities like read, nap, or daydream. But, for the most part, I just love being in my studio and getting to work and don't really spend much time 'setting a mood.' I have a honey-scented candle that has a wonderful fragrance even without being lit that adds to the mood of my studio. When I do remember to put on music, I find that it changes and enhances the environment. And then I usually associate what I was working on with a certain piece of music or musician."

Pam mentions the same thing: "Music in my studio is

hugely important. I listen to a wide variety of alternative, jazz, retro, rock, punk, and electronica music. But I don't skip around between styles during the day. Sometimes I'll listen to the same album or artist over and over during a project. It kind of puts me in a trance, or what I call 'the zone,' so if some music is working to get me there, I don't change until I change projects or media."

Pam goes on to describe her daily routine. "Before I even get to the studio—since I work away from home—I have some little morning tricks to remind myself that I am and want to remain creative throughout the day. My brother calls me Mr. Rogers, because I dress nicely to get to the studio, then often change my sweater and shoes at the studio to work. But I have a collection of cartoon and graphic watches that I wear, kind of a signal to remind me that 'it's time to be creative.' Also I like to start the day with coffee or tea from a handmade mug, of which we have a big assortment. It reminds me of some other artists I know who made the mug, or some art event or some other place that we bought it. Sometimes I take off my shoes to feel more creative.

"Lately, I've been not checking the e-mail at home in the morning because it can really stall out my day. Right now I'm trying to get to the studio

by 9AM—that's after workout, breakfast and tasks at home—and do something creative and important before I check the e-mail. When I get to the studio, I start by turning on music, lighting a bit of incense and making an entry into my sketchbook. It's a simple entry, with a day or date and a short list of things that I want to accomplish for the day. Then on the side of that, I do some sort of drawing, quick painting or collage. It's a chance to just totally experiment. It doesn't have to be very good, you see, because it's just part of my to-do list, so I don't really have any inhibitions. And the to-do list has to be

Mackenzie—Lori Sandstedt

131

short and do-able, because it's part of the drawing and I don't want a lot of unfinished business messing up my drawing. And after I do that page, I feel totally released and ready to focus on the work.

"I'm trying to incorporate more rituals like that into my life, because if you look at Japanese art, such as ikebana, tea ceremony and calligraphy, there is a lot of ritual in preparing the place and materials and equipment. What they are really doing is preparing the mind to be in the proper mood to be spontaneous and yet studied and skillful all at the same time."

Expulsion—Roz Stendahl

She came and put her chin down on the flat file and just looked so mystified and forlorn. The girls both loved harmonica music, like I do, and would sing along with me—mostly, I think, to drown me out. A break for a rousing round of sing-along harmonica playing is something I still miss."

At first glance, Roz seems like a true minimalist: She doesn't eat or drink in the studio. Most of the time—"99.9 percent of the time"—she works in complete silence. No fountains, no wind chimes. Nothing. No odors—she has allergies and asthma. For Roz, it's all about the work. And there you'll find the little hidden rituals she uses to prepare herself for the long (happy) hours she spends working.

Roz says, "I typically work in silence—that is, the white noise generated by the computer equipment, or the noise of traffic and life happening outside. I even do this when binding. But there are some times when I do turn on the music. Typically it is when I'm very stressed because the computer has started to act weird and I need to meet a deadline. In those situations I put in a CD of Gregorian chants or listen to a CD of R. Carlos Nakai. Both these types of music have a soothing effect on me—the same effect, in fact, of lying next to an 80-pound Alaskan Malamute who is napping, and listening to her quiet breathing. No other music will work this way. I get calm pretty fast and then turn it off the next time I get up to stretch my legs, which is at least every thirty minutes.

"Once I tried a 'wolves calling in the rainy forest' CD, and that was a huge mistake. Emma [*author note: one of the two Alaskan Malamutes who were her constant companions*] was already dead, but Dottie was still alive.

"I have little rituals for working in any media, if you count setting up; and I suppose you have to. I like to be productive and efficient, so I've worked out ways to set up my workspace when I watercolor, or tear papers, or bind books, etc. When I teach these activities, I teach these setups as a way for people to begin and then find their own way to be productive. I think it's as simple as wanting things where I want them when I need them. Work then just becomes one fluid motion.

"When I work in colored pencils, I develop a palette for the drawing I'm working on; and then, if it is a large drawing with large areas that will need covering, I get several pencils of each color I'm going to use and sharpen them all at once. This has to do with the way I work with colored pencils: I take lots of small strokes. By the

Expulsion Materials—Roz Stendahl

time one pencil's point isn't useful, I go on to another, and another. Then I take a break and sharpen five to ten more pencils at one time. It also gives my eyes a break from all the close work.

"Another habit I have is that I will work on one job and then take a break from it by working on another job of a different sort. So I might work on a gouache painting of a rock in the morning when my eyes are fresh and I can do the detail work, and then take a break and do some basket weaving, or tear some paper down for making books. Then I go back to yet another job or return to the first one if my eyes feel rested.

"I also like to use 'free' moments to work in my journal. This isn't always about drawing or painting an object or scene on the page. Sometimes I take a break in my day just to paint pages in my journals so that there will be a 'background' there when I get to that page, days or even weeks later."

Whether your studio rituals are the obvious kind—putting out the studio flag, lighting a particular candle, putting on a certain CD—or the more work-habit ones like Roz's, what's important is that they work for you. Whatever little habits and tricks you can use to help make the shift from The World Out There to the world in your studio space are all good. Experiment: Try some of the music, sample some of the tea. When you find one that seems to spark that creative mood, make time for it in your daily routine. And if that routine sometimes begins to seem a little stale? Ah—then maybe it's time to take it on the road.

Chapter 10

Taking It on the Road

Sometimes You Really *Can* Take It With You

Having a wonderful studio, whatever its size and shape, is a Good Thing. But sometimes you need to get away. Whether it's a long-awaited, much-needed vacation or an afternoon spent at the local coffee house, time away from the studio can fill your brain with fresh ideas and give you a new perspective on everything from art to business. So you'd think that artists would jump at the chance to take some time off, or at least time away from where they work, right? But when you love what you do, the idea of "time off" isn't always that appealing. How do artists feel about getting away from work? Well, some of them do it well: Listen to Pam.

"Relaxing is an important part of being creative, so I do try to relax in different ways—by yoga, exercise, hot baths, massages, and vacations. I think being relaxed opens a portal to your subconscious and new ideas." She and her husband try to get away regularly throughout the year, as do Lori and her husband. Lori explains, "My husband and I take a couple trips a year, and I enjoy getting away from my work for a while. I love immersing myself in a new culture and getting recharged. It's not like I forget what I do and leave it all behind—I'm busy taking everything in, and the inspiration travel provides finds its way into my work when I get back home. I have found that I truly miss my studio if I'm gone for more than about ten to twelve days. That's about the maximum time

Wide Life, Love—Kelly Rae Roberts

I can be away without feeling a little pain of withdrawal." For most of the other artists, a fraction of that time is about all they can stay away. Traci, who's always traveling anyway, says, "I usually take two to three days to visit friends, family, or new cities to explore when I am on the road. I like to make sure I take time for relaxation. It's important to me to do this, since my schedule and business endeavors take up so much of my days. There are days when I don't answer my phone or check my e-mail and just take a 'me' day."

Axis—Thomas Mann

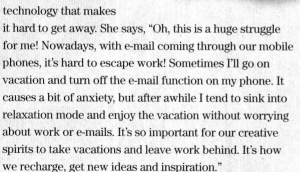

135

For Kelly, too, it's technology that makes it hard to get away. She says, "Oh, this is a huge struggle for me! Nowadays, with e-mail coming through our mobile phones, it's hard to escape work! Sometimes I'll go on vacation and turn off the e-mail function on my phone. It causes a bit of anxiety, but after awhile I tend to sink into relaxation mode and enjoy the vacation without worrying about work or e-mails. It's so important for our creative spirits to take vacations and leave work behind. It's how we recharge, get new ideas and inspiration."

For many people, a vacation isn't so much a chance to do nothing as it is to do some of what you usually do, but with different scenery. Chris says, "I am always working, but when I go on vacation, I leave everything at home—even though I usually regret not bringing something with me."

Teesha has a completely different take on the idea of taking vacations and relaxing. She says, "If we went on a vacation strictly for relaxing, it would *have* to involve art, because art *does* relax us, even more so than doing nothing does. And that is why, when people tell me that they are so stressed out after work that they can't make art, I roll my eyeballs. They haven't made the connection yet that making art re-energizes you way more than zombie-ing out in front of the TV. Based on recent reading from Eckhart Tolle, I am only now understanding why. It is because you are in the moment when you create, and that is what makes one feel the most alive. To me, 'work' is the business side of art. To actually make the art is like playing. That is why I feel so blessed to do what I am doing."

Carter says, "I can take vacations for relaxing, but it doesn't happen very often. Mostly because I get to go to so many cool places for work, I like to stay home when I can. With Bead Trust I do a lot of bead shows, so I get to go to places like New York, Hawaii, Florida, Texas—all over. And I have even had the opportunity to travel to China! In fact, during the summer I travel so much for work that it's more like a vacation to stay home."

Tom feels the same way: "Vacations—well, they're rare these days, but there are weekends here and there where I get to go away to the beach and chill for a couple of days. But mostly just the fact of being home in my house is like a vacation, so I'll go into the studio late and come home early for a couple of days and treat it like a vacation. If I do get to 'go on vacation,' I'll more than likely

What Kind of Vacation Do You Need?

In your notebook, make a list of the last half-dozen vacations you've taken, even if you have to reach all the way back to childhood to list that many. If you take a lot of vacations, list more. Now take a look at them and think about which ones felt creative, where you either worked on a project or got ideas for a new piece or somehow spent time in a way that recharged your art when you came back home. Circle those, and then think about what it was about those trips that inspired your creativity. Was is the location? The people you were with? How you spent your days or what you saw? That's what you want more of when you travel, whether it's around the globe or just down the highway.

Travel Journals

A travel journal is a great place to collect all the ideas and inspiration from a trip, whether it's out of the country or down the road to the state fair. Roz says, "Typically I will take a special trip journal that I've made for the occasion. I like to just have things relating to the trip in a particular journal. I've always done this my entire life, and I don't know any other way to take a trip." She mentions the fun of picking the format and the paper and designing the structure and cover, and she adds, "There is also the fun and excitement of packing the art supplies." Whether you bind your own journal or buy a new spiral notebook, having a separate journal for each trip encourages you to fill it up with everything you see and hear and think about while you're away from home. Then, when you're back home, you have that whole volume, clearly labeled, to provide endless inspiration.

take a little kit of tools along, some bits of wire, little screws, a hand drill—so I can make things out of stuff I find in the environment of the vacation spot."

That's pretty much the way it is for most artists: No matter where they are or what they're supposed to be doing (relaxing, sight-seeing, visiting), their creative brains are sucking in ideas and inspiration, working away in the background.

Judy Wise says, "I do go on vacations, and I leave the manual part of the work behind, but of course I am photographing, writing, gathering collage material and so on for when I get home. Then I create art from my photos."

Traveling with Others

If you usually travel with other people—colleagues, family, children, a partner—you have to adapt your plans to theirs. While it might mean that you don't get to spend the entire two weeks traveling from one workshop to another, it doesn't mean your vacation can't be about art. Listen to Roz:

"I don't have any trouble traveling with people who have different goals because I only travel with people who know me, and so they know what I'll be doing. Either they are the type of people who are also keeping journals, or they are the type of people who are so into 'vacation' mode that the aspect of me doing my thing is not at all a bother to them. I don't require that people stop while I sketch, for instance—instead I find ways to work very fast in the opportune moments that arise. That's the fun of traveling with others." If your kids want to go swimming? Perfect for sketching swimmers in the pool or trying out a few watercolor images. Partner wants to play golf? Spring for the cart and sit in the shade and work on capturing the light reflecting off the grass and sand.

[Author's note: Don't worry that this will make you a pain to your companions. I've traveled with Roz, and this is exactly what she does: No matter what you're doing, she's happily sketching and making notes about it, from meals to longhorn cattle on the side of the highway. Her sketching habit makes her the most charming of traveling companions—her curiosity is stimulating, and you can always count on her to have notes that will lead you back to that out-of-the-way café with the fabulous ice cream.]

Roz adds, "I don't know what it would be like to sit on a beach and just read a book and soak up the sun. I might sit on that beach, but I'm always thinking about something, like how I can turn those shells into a necklace; or I am painting or thinking about geology, or weather, or water quality, and asking myself 10,000 questions that I want answered when I get home and have access to reference materials. I am able to leave client work behind when I go on trips. Typically this is easy to do because I schedule my work so that it is all out of the office when I need to be gone. But my personal work, my visual and written journaling, is never left behind. I'm always thinking of new series of paintings I want to do, new jewelry I want to make, new baskets, a new book structure. I like to get them down in the journal as soon as they pop up. There is also the part of me that sees travel as a disruption of my productivity. I'm usually not keen on going places—perhaps because I've already been a lot of places. Once I get going, however, I'm pretty happy with the experience, even if it is full of problems."

Judy Perez says, "I can't imagine not thinking about making art while on vacation. It would be impossible for me to look at sand and seashells without being inspired by their shapes and colors and wanting to draw them."

And then there are those who don't even try to take vacations, at least not in the way most of us think of them. Whether it's time constraints or the demands of work or just the fact that there's no reason for them to get away from something they love, some artists express shock at the very idea of A Vacation.

Theo says, "I'm a bit of a workaholic, I suppose. I have a hard time taking even one full day off. I take moments off. I'm working on relaxing more and taking more time to recharge. I seem to have too many things going on at once; so I'm trying to prioritize, to put my focus on the truly important projects and allow myself to let go of the things that aren't pushing me forward in a bigger way. I took a full day off for the very first time in a very long time a little while ago. My girlfriend and I went riding bikes all over Portland, and we discovered some amazing bike trails that I didn't know about before. Then I made my famous enchiladas, and we drank red wine and watched movies. Having a total play day like that was thrilling! I feel lucky to be making a living doing what I love, so it's taken me a while to get my head around the concept of 'taking a day off from doing the thing that you love.' A day where I don't draw is usually an off day for me. But

Violinist & Bird—Judy Wise

as I get further into it, I find myself wanting to shape my time to allow for hours of intensive focus each day, then leave my studio and rejoin the world for a while. I think the hours spent not working are an important part of the creative whole. I think I'm getting there."

Lisa says, "When I am forced to go on vacation, I find it endless. Two days and I am dying to get back to the studio. When I do business trips, it is the same thing. Still, seeing new faces and places is stimulating. I can't imagine leaving 'being an artist' behind and see no need escaping it unless I am having a nervous breakdown or something."

Susan was shocked at the very idea of vacations. She says, "Take a vacation? I haven't had one of those since I became a full-time artist in 2000. When we gave up my salary—a teaching job—that was one of the things we knew that would suffer. We try and take a weekend here and there, but I work it around art-related stuff. I might be visiting galleries, having a show or teaching a class. That way I can write the trip off on my taxes. I am hoping that I will be able to start taking some time away from the studio so I can just sit and read. I love to travel and see new places and cultures and I really miss that."

Whether it's a Real Vacation, with swimsuits and a passport, or just a trip to your favorite coffee house, there's always the question of whether or not you take it with you—"it" being a project, your laptop, your sketchbook—whatever it is that you do.

Lisa says, "The nature of working with nylon makes it impossible to take with me on trips. I would like to do some painting outdoors—I always loved to do that but never have the time. I think it would be relaxing. I used to bring my sketchbook everywhere until I trained my brain to record what I see so I could sketch it later. That has been very useful, although it only works with certain faces or things that really strike me as extremely interesting."

Judy Wise says, "I am not a person who works on the road. When I travel, I travel. Maybe at some point I'll collage and write in my journal, but I can't imagine wanting to haul stuff around to work on. Having said that, I'll admit to once buying a set of watercolors in Hawaii because I missed them and wanted to paint. But only that one time. Usually my camera is enough to keep me entertained." The camera works like that for lots of artists—not only does it record the usual snapshots of places and people but it also captures colors and images, line and texture, ideas and possibilities. Combine those with notes written in your notebook, and you'll never run out of inspiration.

Lori says, "I don't carry my work with me, nor do I know how to sketch. So that pretty much eliminates me continuing to work when I'm outside the studio. That doesn't mean I don't think about it when I'm out and about—I may make some notes in a small journal or take photographs of things that inspire me. Photography becomes my creative outlet when I travel."

Pam says, "I think of travel as the elixir of creativity. It doesn't contribute so much to a specific project, so I don't try to take one with me. It's more the general getting out of a current mind-set, or opening myself to new experiences, people, ideas, ways of working, or other customs that contribute to me rethinking and re-forming my own life when I return home. I always carry a sketchbook and a few drawing supplies when I'm just out and about, especially if I'm going to the dentist or to get my oil changed because those moments when I'm trapped in a waiting room are moments that can be used. On long trips, I'll take sketchbooks, art supplies, laptop and cameras. I always

Theo Ellsworth

take tons of photographs when traveling. Later I'll study the photos, especially photos of other artists' workspaces, because with the photos, I sometimes notice more than I did in real life. However, in museums and galleries, sometimes you can't take photos. Often when I do a little sketch of a work of art, I notice more about the work—I guess because I'm processing it through my drawing brain and trying to re-create it, so in that case, I get more benefit from the drawing than a photo."

Judy Perez says, "When I travel, I always bring a sketchbook with watercolor pencils, and knitting. My camera is another way I document images when I am away from home. I carry a little Moleskine sketchbook in my purse to jot notes and sketch ideas when I am out and about. I often come up with ideas while I am driving or waiting for my kids to finish one of their classes, or waiting for a doctor's appointment."

Carter says, "It's not easy to pack up all of my stringing tools and beads, and pretty impossible to travel with my torch. So I try to travel with the paper tasks. I always have something that I can work on on the computer."

Traci says, "I like the term 'creative journeys'—that sums up my life on a daily basis. Since I travel so much, I have learned to work everywhere. I enjoy working outside of my studio. I work in hotel rooms, friends' houses, coffee shops, on airplanes, in the airport . . . With the access to technology via my iPhone, I can check e-mail, make phone calls, take photos, update my blog, find a local Kinko's on the road, make airline reservations, and IM with a touch of a button. I carry a notebook-sketchbook for my lists; sometimes I'll doodle in them or collect ideas for artwork. Travel for me both stimulates and hinders my work. Being on the road is great inspiration for writing, researching, designing, and networking, but the travel time and being away from the studio also keeps me from creating artwork on a regular basis."

Teesha says, "I take my journal with me wherever I go. But I only take some pens unless I am going away for a long time. Then I will take collage, scissors, tape, crayons and so on. I might also bring small 'pillows' that are lightly stuffed, and some embroidery floss and a needle for impromptu hand quilting while sitting in a hotel room, if journaling just isn't what I feel like doing. Later, the pillows can be attached to each other and can be turned into anything I want to make."

You can see that, for most of our artists, the size and nature of their work—wall quilts, soldered glass, life-sized figurative sculpture—prohibits working on it at the coffee shop while sipping a latte and visiting with friends. For those who work smaller, though, taking the work out of the studio provides a nice break.

Susan says, "I am constantly dragging my stitching with me when I go on trips or to appointments. I have taken it on planes, on a cruise and in the car. I don't like having time like that on my hands without utilizing it. If I don't have my handwork, I am reading some type of art or creativity book. When I am on car trips with my husband, I am completely happy stitching away and listening to music—and it makes my husband happy that I am not backseat driving. When I am in a public place, people will ask me what I am doing, and it gives me a chance to talk about fiber art and my work."

Paper and pen offer the utmost in portability. While most artists carry their journal or sketchbook with them,

Working in Public

If you're just the tiniest bit uncomfortable working in public, you're certainly not alone. Rather than looking at it from the inside and noticing your discomfort at being so exposed, so out there, try looking at it from the outside: You're this fascinating person doing something cool and out of the ordinary. If you set up a table with watercolors or your journal, you're creating a chance to expose someone else to the joy you find in being creative. Be willing to answer questions and provide encouragement. You never know what other artist might come by, love the idea of working in public, and start up regular art meetings.

Theo's paper and pen are his actual work. He explains, "I take my work wherever I go. It can be harder to work while I'm traveling, but I've discovered that if I come up with a spontaneous project I can do while I'm traveling, I can usually be prolific. Travel is always stimulating to me—I love to travel! It's been getting harder to find the time. Most of my traveling over the last couple of years has been art related. I always come back to my studio really fired up to get back to work. I like drawing in coffee shops, but I never think to do it on my own. I love meeting friends at coffee shops and drawing. I hang out with my girlfriend at coffee shops a lot and draw while she studies Chinese medicine. If it's just me, I'd usually rather be in my studio where I can have a more intense focus."

Roz says, "My journal is always with me regardless of where I'm going. So in that sense my work is always with me. But I don't take work out of the studio that has lots of fussy bits—beading, weaving, jewelry making. I don't want

Portfolio—Pam RuBert

to lose things; I don't want things to get dirty. The fact that travel takes me out of my usual routine yet allows me to do all the things I love doing—observing and sketching in my journal—makes it ultimately a good thing."

Wherever you go—down the hall to your kitchen table, out into the garage to your workbench, around the country on a teaching tour—your art goes with you. Sometimes it's the tangible piece in progress, and sometimes it's between the pages of your sketchbook. As you make time and space for the art you love, you'll find it flowing into the routines of your days and adding joy to even the most mundane tasks. If Pam's little drawings can transform a daily to-do list into an experiment with a new set of paints, think what your own creative habits will do to the routines in your own life. Go. Create. Enjoy!

Index

About Ricë

Ricë Freeman-Zachery lives in Midland, Texas, because the weather is warm and the mortgage is cheap. Her name rhymes with *Lisa* and no, her hair is not naturally orange.

Having answered those three most-asked questions, she'd like to add that she is well aware of her incredibly good fortune in getting to spend her days doing things she's loved most since childhood: writing, making things from nothing, and attempting to make people laugh. Also, herding cats and hanging out with her boyfriend, who also happens—very conveniently—to be her husband of thirty-three years. Not to mention nagging her various editors for more work so she has an excuse to call up yet more artists and ask them all sorts of nosy questions and, if she's really lucky, travel to their studios.

She'd be ever so happy if you'd stop by and visit her and her friends at www.voodoonotes.blogspot.com.

Photo—Earl Zachery

Indulge Your Creative Side With These Other North Light Titles

Living the Creative Life

Ricë Freeman-Zachery

Living the Creative Life answers your questions about creativity: What is creativity anyway? Where do ideas come from? How do successful artists get started? How do you know when a piece is finished? Author Ricë Freeman-Zachery has compiled answers to these questions and more from 15 successful artists in a variety of mediums—from assemblage to fiber arts, beading to mixed-media collage. This in-depth guide to creativity is full of ideas and insights from inspiring artists, shedding light on what it takes to make art that you want to share with the world, and simply live a creative life.

ISBN-10: 1-58180-994-8 • ISBN-13: 978-1-58180-994-7 • paperback with flaps • 8" × 8" • 144 pages • Z0949

Taking Flight

Kelly Rae Roberts

In *Taking Flight*, you'll find overflowing inspiration—complete with a kindred spirit in author and mixed-media artist Kelly Rae Roberts. Join her on a fearless journey into the heart of creativity as you test your wings and learn to find the sacred in the ordinary, honor your memories, speak your truth and wrap yourself in the arms of community. Along the way you'll be inspired by step-by-step techniques, thought-provoking prompts and quotes and plenty of eye candy—pages and pages of the author's endearing artwork, along with the varied works of the contributors.

ISBN-10: 1-60061-082-X • ISBN-13: 978-1-60061-082-0 • paperback • 8" × 10" • 128 pages • Z1930

Exhibition 36

Susan Tuttle

Jam-packed with visual eye candy, *Exhibition 36* features a plethora of artistic techniques, tips and inspiration from 36 amazing contributing artists. This virtual gallery includes "guest speakers," hands-on workshops and plenty of full-color food for thought. Whether you're looking for painting tips, advice for facing your artistic fears, new tricks for creating digital art or inspiring stories of the challenges artists just like you face, you'll find something of value on every page of this amazing collection of creative food for the soul.

ISBN-10: 1 [31901050122037] k • 8" × 10" • 160 pages • Z2065

These books and other fine North Light titles are available at your local craft retailer, bookstore or online supplier, or visit us at www.mycraftivitystore.com.